GLEB USPENSKY

TWAYNE'S WORLD AUTHORS SERIES

A Survey of the World's Literature

Sylvia E. Bowman, Indiana University

GENERAL EDITOR

RUSSIA

Nicholas P. Vaslef, U. S. Air Force Academy

EDITOR

Gleb Uspensky

(TWAS 190)

TWAYNE'S WORLD AUTHORS SERIES (TWAS)

The purpose of TWAS is to survey the major writers —novelists, dramatists, historians, poets, philosophers, and critics—of the nations of the world. Among the national literatures covered are those of Australia, Canada, China, Eastern Europe, France, Germany, Greece, India, Italy, Japan, Latin America, New Zealand, Poland, Russia, Scandinavia, Spain, and the African nations, as well as Hebrew, Yiddish, and Latin Classical literatures. To provide a truly international focus, foreign scholars have been invited to participate in the writing of these books. This survey is complemented by Twayne's United States Authors Series and English Authors Series.

The intent of each volume in these series is to present a critical-analytical study of the works of the writer; to include biographical and historical material that may be necessary for understanding, appreciation, and critical appraisal of the writer; and to present all material in clear, concise English—but not to vitiate the scholarly content of the work by doing so.

Gleb Uspensky

By NIKITA I. PRUTSKOV

Academy of Sciences of the USSR

Prepared for publication by the Novosti Press Agency (APN)
Publishing House, USSR

Twayne Publishers, Inc. :: New York

To

NATALIE PRUTSKOV

"...he writes the truth, and from this truth
emerges the tragic truth about Russian life..."
M. E. Saltykov (N. Shchedrin),
False Misgivings (1868)

Preface

Gleb Ivanovich Uspensky (1843-1902) was unique as an individual. He had enormous artistic talents; his insights into the life of his time were often brilliant and penetrating. His works, original in form, remain significant for our time, both socially and morally. The most important are: *Manners of Rasteryaeva Street, Ruin, From a Village Diary, Peasant and Peasant Labor, The Power of the Soil, Vypryamila, Willy-Nilly,* "Checkbook," *Living Figures,* and "Bitter Reproach."

Uspensky belonged to the distinguished generation of Russian Populist-Democrats of the second half of the nineteenth century. His knowledge of the Russian village and his vivid descriptions of the manners, psychology, and outlook of the peasant of old Russia have earned him a secure place in world literature. Without reading Uspensky one can have but an incomplete understanding of the pre-revolutionary Russian village, its sufferings, and hopes. Uspensky's own innermost hopes were closely linked to the Russian village.

He was a Peasant Socialist-Utopian who searched for ways of establishing "heavenly truth" on earth and social harmony in life. He wanted to see the perfect, all-round development of man. In seeking for "materials" with which to build his social and moral ideal, Uspensky—unlike Dostoevsky—did not turn to the "Golden Age" or the "children of the sun," but to the living "example" of his ideals—the Russian peasant who lived by the labor of his hands and the Russian revolutionary who embodied the spirit of self-sacrifice. Uspensky also found a similar example in the Venus of Milo, for in Uspensky's mind the Russian peasant, Russian revolutionary, and the ancient goddess were curiously and wonderfully merged into one. This phenomenon is unique in world literature and could have appeared only on Russian soil, though it possesses universal significance.

Foreword

In his fantasy, *Shadows*, Vladimir Korolenko has Socrates say defiantly to the Olympian gods:

> ... I am no builder, no creator of a new temple. I was not destined to raise on the old site the majestic edifice of the new faith. For I am only a dustman, moving among the debris left after the demolition. But my conscience tells me that the work of a dustman is also necessary for the future temple. When on the cleared site there rises, beautifully and majestically, the wonderful structure in which the living god of the new faith is enthroned, I, the humble dustman, shall go to him and say, "Here I am, who have patiently dwelled in the ashes of negation. Surrounded by rubble and dust I had had no time to lift my eyes from the earth; I had only a vague notion of what the future looked like.... Are you going to reject me, you who are righteous, true, and great?"[1]

And indeed, all progressive Russian writers felt like Korolenko's Socrates, a "restless gadfly." The "dustmen of history," who cleared the way for the future, extracting truth and justice from the rubble of the old world which they had torn down, were the makers of Russian literature of the last century. Foremost among them was Gleb Ivanovich Uspensky (1843-1902).

About Uspensky Korolenko wrote: "With feverish passion he searched among the debris of the old for things that could be used in creating the new conscience, for rules for the new life or new quests of this life."[2] Gorky called Uspensky a "very clever man." According to some of his contemporaries, Uspensky was a man of genius who from the very first came into sharp conflict with the semi-feudal, bureaucratic, and Philistine life of his time. It was a hopeless conflict which led to endless suffering, restlessness, and a constant and anxious search for social justice and harmony. The search resulted in a deep spiritual crisis and—eventually—in insanity.

Uspensky had a fine analytical mind. He saw clearly what was happening in Russia following the abolition of serfdom in 1861. He was irresistibly attracted to the new, and his insights into Russian capitalism and what it was doing to the country were often truly brilliant. At the same time, however, there was much about the new order which he did not and could not understand. It disturbed and bewildered him, giving rise to tormenting doubts, fear, despair, as well as some shrewd conjectures. To the end of his life Uspensky retained his love for the peasant of pre-Capitalist Russia, though he knew perfectly well that this peasant of the old type was disappearing under the "iron laws" of the new era. Confused and anxious, Uspensky was torn between the old which he cherished and which seemed to him to be desirable and humane, and the new which he regarded as harsh, merciless, and inhumane. This conflict proved to be tragic for him.

As an artist and a thinker Uspensky was absolutely sincere and honest. He took nothing on faith. In his search for truth he often had to destroy what he loved, though he received nothing or almost nothing in return. He relentlessly shattered his own illusions and hopes and those of others. Uspensky may well be called a "destroyer of illusions," for the ones he exposed were the most popular of his day. By portraying Russian life as it really was, by pointing out the meaning of what was happening in the country, Uspensky helped liberate the minds of many of his contemporaries from their fascination with Populist-Socialist ideals.

Uspensky was extremely inconsistent and unsettled in his ideas, feelings, and moods. He was constantly in search of answers to various intellectual and moral questions, and his conclusions often conflicted with his feelings. But this does not mean that Uspensky was merely an emotional and excitable observer, one who constantly fell into argument with himself and expressed his opinions unconvincingly. While it is true that a tone of bewildered and anguished questioning and reproach, fear, and even terror of reality is inherent in his style—a style which Gorky characterized as "hysterical lyricism"—this tone is not present in all of Uspensky's works. In some of his writings of the 1870's and 1880's this tone is notable, but secondary; more important is deep-rooted Realism, for Uspensky did not consider that his main task as a writer was to acquaint the readers with his thoughts, doubts, and questions. Instead, what he sought above all was to understand contemporary life and to depict it truthfully. His attempt to do this was marked not only by doubts, dread, and the lyricism of a morbid mind, but also by an analytical passion and convictions that were progressive for his time.

Uspensky courageously championed democratic changes. He was not only a fighter with strong moral convictions, but also a writer and sociologist who tirelessly inquired into the meaning and conditions of life. He was a man of passionate beliefs and opinions, which led him to oppose both the theories prevalent in his time and the programs of the Populist movement.

What is most important and characteristic about the mature Uspensky is to be found in his essays of the 1870's and 1880's. These essays often begin with perplexing questions, with a sense of confusion for that which is portrayed, but the analysis that follows removes the perplexity, penetrates to the heart of the questions, and enables the author to arrive at conclusions and convictions on which his practical solutions are based. Sometimes these solutions give way to new doubts, and the search continues. This entire process can sometimes be traced in a single essay cycle.

In this volume I have dealt with this extremely complex dialectic present in Uspensky's works between doubt and conviction, bewilderment and determination, confusion and affirmation. This dialectic was in a state of constant development and reflected the contradictions of those times.

I have made an analytical study of Uspensky's major works: *The Manners of Rasteryaeva Street, Ruin, Sick Conscience, From a Village Diary, Peasant and Peasant Labor, The Power of the Soil,* "By the Labor of One's Own Hands," *Vypryamila,* and "Bitter Reproach." In discussing the intellectual and artistic conceptions in these works, I try to describe the hopes and disappointment of Uspensky, the contradictions that characterize his works, and the intellectual and psychological causes, as well as the historical significance of Uspensky's final spiritual tragedy.[3]

NIKITA PRUTSKOV

Leningrad, USSR

Contents

Chronology

1843   Gleb Ivanovich Uspensky born October 13, in Tula.

1856   Family moves to Chernigov.

1861   Graduates from Chernigov secondary school. Enters law school of St. Petersburg University in fall. University closed December 20 because of student disturbances. Uspensky expelled.

1862   Enrolls in law school of Moscow University in September. Forced to leave University in April for inability to pay tuition. First works, "Mikhalych" and "Idylls," published.

1864   Father dies unexpectedly shortly after having gone bankrupt. Responsibility of supporting large family falls on Uspensky, the oldest child.

1866   First book, *Sketches and Tales*, published in St. Petersburg.

1866-   Period of literary frustration and financial hardships.
1868

1871   *Sketches and Tales, Ruin*, and other works published.

1871-   Works attract wide critical attention for the first time.
1872

1872   Goes abroad in April. Visits France, Germany, and Belgium. Returns in July.

1873   Placed under police surveillance, which continues until almost end of his life.

1875   Second trip abroad.

1877   Returns from abroad at beginning of year.

1880   March 2, Ivan S. Turgenev, who returned from Paris previous winter, and group of young writers meet in Uspensky's apartment in suburb of St. Petersburg. Uspensky and G. Eliseev attend the Pushkin celebrations in Moscow, June 5-8, as representatives of the journal *Otechestvennye zapiski*.

1881   New Year's eve gathering with leading members of *Narodnaya volya* in Uspensky's apartment in St. Petersburg.

1882   Works (*Rural Disorder*, in 3 volumes) included in the *Library of Contemporary Writers* series for the first time.

1883   January-March. Journey to Caucasus. Elected active member of the *Obshchestvo lyubiteley rossiyskoy slovesnosti* (Society of Lovers of Russian Literature) at Moscow University. Collected works in 8 volumes begin to be published by F. Pavlenkov in St. Petersburg.

1884   Publication of *Otechestvennye zapiski* (to which Uspensky contributed) is stopped by authorities in April. Uspensky loses regular source of income.

1887   November, receives congratulatory messages from all parts of Russia on occasion of 25th anniversary of his debut as a writer.

1888   June, goes on long-planned journey to Siberia. December 3, new 2-volume edition of Uspensky's works published (10,000 copies printed) with introductory essay "Gleb Uspensky, a literary portrait" by N. K. Mikhaylovsky.

1892   Stays in St. Petersburg private mental hospital run by A. Ya. Frey from July to September. Falls into state of depression, tries to maim himself and commit suicide.

1892   September 21, leaves Frey hospital, enters Kolmovskaya mental hospital near Novgorod. Remains there until November 13, 1893 under observation of B. Sinani, famous Russian psychiatrist.

1893   In August, while in Kolmovskaya mental hospital, begins work on his reminiscences about children, Paris, Turgenev, and Vera Figner. Fails to complete work because of illness. Best part of carefully planned work is "My Children." Last work of Uspensky, now seriously ill—"Abandoned Child"—appears in the journal, *Russkoe Bogatstvo*, No. 6. Edition of *Four Stories* published in Moscow.

1900   March 18, leaves Kolmovskaya hospital, enters Novo-Znamenskaya hospital in St. Petersburg.

1902   March 24, dies of heart attack in Novo-Znamenskaya hospital. Buried on March 27 at Volkov Cemetery in St. Petersburg.

CHAPTER 1

Gleb Uspensky: The Man and Writer

> *". . . the purest of hearts, the most noble, a unique person—such was Gleb Uspensky. This pure heart, exhausting itself from concern for the people, died of anguish for the people. I do not know any other writer who has portrayed the peasant so sensitively, with so much pain. . . ."*
>
> Alexander S. Serafimovich,
> *Writer and the People* (1917)

I *"The Turbulent Years"*

THE works of Gleb Ivanovich Uspensky appeared between the 1860's and the 1880's, at a time of great social and political turmoil in Russia. It was the eve of the abolition of serfdom, and the years between 1859 and 1861 marked a period in which a revolutionary situation was beginning to emerge.

The Crimean War (1853-56) exposed the corruption and the weaknesses of the autocratic regime and aggravated the crisis in which the regime found itself, leading to unrest among the masses and shaking the intellectual and literary world. After the war, the abolition of serfdom became an urgent national issue. The best people in the country waited impatiently for the explosion of the people's anger and were ready to take an active part in the coming peasants' revolution. At the end of 1860 the journal *Sovremennik* (*The Contemporary*), edited by Nikolay A. Nekrasov, published a stirring article by two Populist-Democrat Socialists—Nikolay G. Chernyshevsky and Nikolay A. Dobrolyubov—whose writings had inspired all radical literature of the time.

The revolutionary situation became tense in 1861 when village reforms were put into effect. In 1861-62 approximately fifteen hundred peasant revolts were reported. There was good reason for this. While the tsar's Manifesto of February

17

19, 1861 formally abolished serfdom, the peasants gained little from it. They were, in fact, shamelessly robbed, since most of the land and the best land remained in the possession of the gentry. Nor were the peasants granted any real civil or political rights. What the people had eagerly awaited after centuries of slavery had failed to come about. As Korolenko noted: "The great reform stirred up the nation's entire life, but the wave of regeneration soon began to recede. What should have fallen did not fall in the end; what should have risen did not rise at all."[1]

In 1862 the democratic movement began to decline and peasant revolts were cruelly repressed. After putting down these disorders, the authorities turned their attention to the progressive intelligentsia—to the periodicals and to literature. A wave of arrests followed: On July 7, 1862 the leader of the revolutionary intelligentsia, Chernyshevsky, was arrested and imprisoned in the Peter and Paul Fortress. Among others arrested were the critic Dmitry I. Pisarev, the revolutionary Nikolay A. Serno-Solovyovich, and the poet and revolutionary Mikhail L. Mikhaylov. The best journals of the day, Sovremennik and Russkoe slovo (The Russian Word), were forced to cease publication for eight months; in 1866 their publication was stopped altogether.

But the struggle went on. In conditions of rampant reaction a secret revolutionary society, Zemlya i volya (Land and Liberty), was formed,[2] its members inspired by the ideas of Chernyshevsky, Alexander Herzen, and Nikolay P. Ogaryov. In January, 1863 the Polish revolt for national emancipation broke out, which was ruthlessly suppressed. Between 1863 and 1866 a clandestine student group was active in Moscow, which made plans for freeing Chernyshevsky from imprisonment. Some of the members concluded that in order to overthrow the autocratic regime and awaken the revolutionary spirit of the masses it was necessary to kill Tsar Alexander II. One of them, Dmitry V. Karakozov, made an unsuccessful attempt on the tsar's life on April 4, 1866. The incident touched off a new wave of repression directed by Count Mikhail N. Muravyov who was responsible for quelling the Polish revolt. Karakozov was hanged, but the revolutionary intelligentsia fought on. Toward the end of the 1860's there were outbreaks of student disturbances in St.

Petersburg. In the 1870's and 1880's the Populist-Revolutionaries spread the ideas of revolution and socialism among the masses; later they organized the assassination of the tsar.

Thus, the mid-1850's of the last century marked the beginning of a new epoch in the history of Russia, of the movement for emancipation, and of literature. Russian literature of the second half of the nineteenth century developed amidst the turmoil and change accompanying the consolidation of the capitalist social-economic order. It was the epoch in which the seeds of the future Russian revolution were sown.

A new attitude emerged among the masses toward life, man, the social system, the tsar, and religion. Before the abolition of serfdom, the thinking of the Russian people was bound up with faith in God, in the tsar and in every kind of authority. Their spiritual and moral outlook, as well as their family and social relations were unshaken by doubts or critical questioning. They did not concern themselves with questions of human dignity or of the rights, interests, and freedom of the individual. The very idea of the individual and his well-being was nonexistent; everything was subordinated to the nation of autocracy. Generations of ordinary people grew up with the belief that they ought to deny their individuality. This was excellently demonstrated in the works of Uspensky and Saltykov-Shchedrin. And as Korolenko said in his brilliant work, *The History of My Contemporary* (*Istoriya moego sovremennika*), such people explained everything as the "will of God"—an attitude that lay at the spiritual basis of Russian absolutism.

All this began to change in 1861. The liberating reform of that year excited high hopes and expectations throughout Russia. The country's progression from the epoch of serfdom to that of capitalism gave rise to a yearning for national regeneration; it awakened thoughts and hopes that had long lain in slumber. The peasant, too, became a new person, as many old and harmful illusions began to lose their hold on him. He was no longer the ignorant, downtrodden serf who placed his faith in priests, who feared every kind of authority, and who had no sense of his own worth as a human being. The reform gave him hope for owning his own land, for freedom, for liberation from his rapacious masters, for self-government, and for education. Though these aspirations of the peasant were not satisfied by the reform, the thought that he could have a better life never left him again.

The awakening in the peasant of the feeling of personal worth and dignity—a phenomenon to which Uspensky paid special attention—was an extremely significant historical process which eventually led the toiling masses of Russia to struggle for their liberation. This process of awakening was facilitated by the social-economic order that came into being following the reform of 1861 and by the new labor conditions and life of the working people. The younger generation of peasants went through the difficult, but necessary experience of doing seasonal work, living in cities, and working in factories. This experience acquainted many of peasant origin with urban life, broadened their outlook, and instilled in them a sense of solidarity and collectivism.

In the second half of the nineteenth century basic changes occurred in the thinking and moods of the progressive intelligentsia in Russia, in the character of its struggle, and in the social composition of the participants in the literary-social movement. A new period—that of bourgeois democrats or *raznochintsy*—began in the history of the revolutionary-liberation movement, of social thought, criticism, science, literature, and art.

The *raznochintsy* (from *razno-*, meaning "various" and *chiny*, meaning "ranks"), were educated men from the lower classes and strata of Russian society, that is, from families of peasants and petty officials, impoverished gentry, rural priests, and the petty-bourgeoisie. Among them was Uspensky, one of the most knowledgeable of the group and one who most profoundly expressed the ideas, feelings, hopes, and disappointments of the progressive *raznochintsy* who moved among the people and waged a single-handed fight against autocracy.

Calling themselves the "intellectual proletariat," the *raznochintsy* wished to emphasize the fact that they lived modestly by their intellectual labor, chiefly literary work. This ideal of living by one's own labor was clearly expressed by Dmitry Pisarev, a literary critic and one of the leaders of the radical *raznochintsy*, in his article "Thinking Proletariat" (Myslyashehy proletariat) about Chernyshevsky's novel *What Is to Be Done?* (*Chto delat'?*) which was a kind of program for the Russian *raznochintsy*.

The *raznochintsy* eagerly followed every new development in world science and art, and creatively put to use all achievements in the social, intellectual, and artistic fields. The first popularizers of Marxism in Russia were the *raznochintsy*. Some of them had personal contacts with Marx and Engels; they took part in the work of the First International and fought on the barricades of the Paris Commune.

Especially significant is the *raznochintsy*'s relation to the toiling masses of Russia, a relation which came to a tragic end, but which was nonetheless admirable in its own way. The *raznochintsy* understood the people from whom they came; they were able to enter into their feelings and express their moods, pain, and hopes. In this sense the *raznochintsy* were much closer to the people than the aristocratic revolutionaries who took part in the December uprising of 1825. The *raznochintsy* inspired selfless devotion to the people. Their striving "to go to the people" was already taking roots in the mid-1860's and in the next ten years it took on a popular, heroic character, seizing the imagination of many writers and poets, and came to be known as "Populism." The participants in this movement regarded "being among the people" as not only having social, revolutionary-emancipatory, and Socialist significance, but as a moral duty—an act of purging themselves from the evils of serfdom and aristocratic traditions. The *raznochintsy* were people with a special sense of moral responsibility; they were full of Romantic enthusiasm and were entirely selfless; only such people could become inspiring examples of total devotion to the people.

In their revolutionary-emancipatory struggle, their striving to derive strength from the people, to draw close to them, and become one with them, the *raznochintsy* emphasized more than just their plebian attitudes. They incorporated these attitudes in their moral philosophy and in their approach to imaginative literature, science, and art. They categorically rejected aristocratic culture, class egoism, and everything else that was part of the system of serfdom. The scornful attitude which prevailed at the time towards individual liberty and development, despotism in the family and in everyday life, moral and political cowardice, different prejudices, and outdated ideals and traditions were all resolutely attacked by the *raznochintsy*. What they respected was labor, physical and mental. Among the *raznochintsy* there was almost a kind of cult of labor, which was regarded as a necessary condition for attaining individual liberty: the achieving by man of an independent way of life in response to the demands of his heart and convictions. This attitude towards labor became a way of life among the *raznochintsy*, also affecting their conceptions of morality, love, family relations, and art. Most of the *raznochintsy* were materialists, atheists, and Socialists.

In 1874-75 the *raznochintsy* went in great numbers to the countryside to spread the ideas of socialism and organize a peasant revolt. This movement was as famous as that of "going to the people." It powerfully attracted Uspensky. The leaders and theoreticians of this movement, and of the revolutionary Populist movement of the 1870's and 1880's as a whole, were the well-known students of social problems—P. L. Lavrov, M. A. Bakunin, and P. N. Tkachev.

Taking over Herzen's idea that in Russia the man of the future was the peasant, the Populists, including Uspensky, developed this theme further. They were convinced that Russia could and should bypass the capitalist stage of development. By basing itself on the *obshchina** Russia could, through a peasants' revolution "in one stroke" do away with the survivals of serfdom and the bourgeois system, and embark on the road to socialism—or so they thought. However, after they had "gone to the people" in the countryside they discovered that the peasants dreamed, not of socialism or the destruction of autocracy, but of land and the means of achieving a better life through democratic rights. Freedom from exploitation by landowners, kulaks, and the government is what the peasants wanted. This discovery brought bitter disappointment to the revolutionary Populists, among them Uspensky. This was vividly and powerfully told in the memoirs of two outstanding Russian revolutionaries of the time: *Memorable Labor* (*Zapechatlenny trud*) by Vera Figner and *Stories of My Life* (*Povesti moey zhizni*) by Nikolay A. Morozov.

But the revolutionaries did not cease to struggle, and at the

---

*the traditional set-up of the Russian village—the peasant *obshchina*, or agrarian communities—embodied a primitive agrarian collectivism.

end of 1876 the clandestine revolutionary-Populist organization, *Zemlya i volya,* was formed, whose members believed that a revolutionary should subordinate his Socialist ideals to the urgent needs of the people. These needs were expressed in the words: *zemyla* (land) and *volya* (liberty). Members of the organization were also convinced that it was the revolutionary's duty to help the people satisfy their daily wants and to fight the abuse of power by village authorities, the rapacity of the kulaks, money-lenders and tavern-keepers, and the despotism of landowners. They concluded that for this purpose revolutionaries needed to stay in the countryside for a prolonged period of time and work as, for example, land surveyors, teachers, clerks, and doctors. In this way they would have daily contacts with the people and thus be able to instill hopes in them, and defend their interests. The movement, however, failed to achieve its goals.

In the autumn of 1879 *Zemlya i volya* split into two factions: *Narodnaya volya* (The Will of the People) and *Cherny peredel* (Black Partition). Members of *Narodnaya volya* embarked on the path of terrorism against the tsar and his most ruthless henchmen. Members of *Cherny peredel* opposed terrorism; they kept to the original program of *Zemlya i volya* and continued to spread the idea of socialism among the peasants and workers.

Members of *Narodnaya volya* regarded successful terrorist acts as a prelude to revolution—to that broad campaign which, in Vera Figner's words, would "run like fire throughout Russia," stir up society, awaken the masses, and draw them into the struggle, creating a threat to autocracy. But these hopes proved to be illusory and unfounded, as some leaders of *Narodnaya volya* came to realize. Thus, the revolutionaries once again failed to arouse the people and make them revolt. Meanwhile a new tsar, Alexander III, succeeded to the throne, following the assassination in 1881 of Alexander II by the revolutionary Andrey I. Zhelyabov. Alexander III dealt mercilessly with the revolutionaries.

The people did not understand and did not support the action of the revolutionary *raznochintsy* and Russian revolutionaries suffered—in Korolenko's words—the "irreparable tragedy of struggling without the backing of the people." This tragedy was also keenly felt by a number of writers, in particular Uspensky. Uspensky's highest hopes and ideals and thoughts on art were connected with the revolutionary movement. He was himself a member of the progressive Russian *raznochintsy*. In his personal fate, his social stand, and his creative work are embodied the innermost thoughts, convictions, and sufferings of the Russian revolutionaries of the 1870's.

II *Youth*

"Sensitive and vibrating, like a string," was how Uspensky's friends described him. When still a young boy Uspensky showed impatience with the evil, deceit, and injustice which he saw around him.

Gleb Uspensky was born on October 25 (13th, according to the old calendar), 1843 in Tula. His family was part of the well-to-do officialdom of the provincial town. Uspensky grew up in an atmosphere of greed, selfishness, parasitism, and corruption. The hypocricy of the life around him, its dreariness and meaninglessness, morally and spiritually enervating, angered and repelled young Uspensky and aroused in him the desire to escape from such an existence—to become free.

The sufferings of the people were deeply felt by young Uspensky. "In my childhood," he wrote in one of his autobiographical pieces, "I saw what miseries the peasants had to endure, and I suffered with them. The bribery that was everywhere, the forced conscription of peasants into the army, the corruption of village elders and scribes, and the miscarriage of justice were all well known to me."[3]

The secondary school in Tula where Uspensky studied up to the fourth grade was located in Khlebnaya Square, where executions were held. The house in which Uspensky's family lived was on Baranava Street (today Turgenev Street), at the end of which stood a jail. Prisoners could be seen marching up the street, sometimes on their way to the scaffold. The gloomy scenes deeply pained young Uspensky, who was observant and highly impressionable. In 1856 his family moved to Chernigov, and Uspensky enrolled in the secondary school there. His relatives recalled how Uspensky often came home with only the shreds of a shirt left on him, for he would tear his shirt to make bandages for beggars.

His extreme sensitivity to injustice and to the sufferings of others influenced Uspensky's entire moral and social outlook. He began to ask the question: why was it that only a few in the world had enough while the rest went hungry? This led him to protest against surroundings in which one's moral sense was lulled, stupefied, and deadened by sentimentalizing over reality. It also led him to consider the question of stolen wealth and of oppression. The desire grew in him to escape from his "fat" comfort, to liberate himself from the power of despots and petty tyranny, and to go where the hungry and destitute lived.

Young Uspensky read widely and came to know the works of Alexander I. Herzen, Vissarion G. Belinsky, Nikolay G. Chernyshevsky, and Nikolay A. Dobrolyubov as well as contemporary writers. In Chernigov he was the leader of a youth circle which published a hand-copied magazine *Molodye Pobegi* (Young Shoots).

In 1861 Uspensky was graduated from the secondary school in Chernigov and enrolled in St. Petersburg University to study law. On December 20th of the same year the university was closed due to student disturbances, and Uspensky was expelled. He then studied for a year at Moscow University, but was forced to leave in April, 1862 because he could not pay the tuition. In that year his father fell ill, and when he died two years later the family was in dire financial straits. The burden of supporting the large family fell on Uspensky.

His first literary works were two sketches (1862): "Mikhalych" which appeared in the magazine *Yasnaya Polyana* published by Leo Tolstoy[4] and "Idyll: Fathers and Sons" which appeared in *Zritel obshchestvennoy zhizni, literatury i sporta* (*Observer of Social Life, Literature and Sports*). From that time on Uspensky devoted himself wholly to literature: "My entire new life, after burying the old, is told almost from day to day in my books; there was and is nothing else in my personal life" (*Autobiography*, XIV, p. 580). Uspensky quickly became part of the literary world and by the late 1860's was a known writer. His talent was recognized by the poet, Nikolay A. Nekrasov, who invited Uspensky to contribute to *Sovremennik* of which he was the editor. The first four chapters of the novel, *Manners of Rasteryaeva Street* (*Nravy Rasteryaevoy ulitsy*), Uspensky's first substantial literary work, appeared in *Sovremennik* (1866). But soon afterwards, publication of *Sovremennik* was suspended by the authorities, and Uspensky was forced to look for other means of livelihood.

In 1867 Uspensky passed the examination required for teachers of Russian language in rural districts and was sent to the town of Epifan (Tula Province). He found the atmosphere there unbearable and a few months later resigned his teaching post and went to Moscow where he took the job of clerk to the Assistant Procurator, Prince A. I. Urusov.

In 1868 Uspensky's literary fortunes took a turn for the better.

III   *To Bury His Past*

The process of embarking on the broad road of life and literature was not an easy one for Uspensky. He first had to, as Maxim Gorky said, "remove from his soul his past life, that is, recollections of that past which in one way or another fell under the corrupt influence of serfdom."[5] Uspensky told about the strain which he underwent in getting rid of this corrupt influence, in his brief autobiographical sketch, written around 1883 for the first 8-volume edition of his work published by F. F. Pavlenko.[6] In it Uspensky told how the surroundings in which he grew up until his twentieth year doomed him to "total obliteration of the mind, total ruin, utter absurdity of opinions and views, intellectual backwardness, and in general separation from the larger world."

That is why it was impossible after 1861 (the year of the abolition of serfdom) for me on my long journey forward to take with me anything from my past . . . ; on the contrary, in order to continue to live at all, I had to forget my entire past, to destroy those qualities which have been instilled in me by this past. . . . Therefore my life began only after I had buried my early life. (XIV, p. 576)

This confession by Uspensky shows the determination with which he strived towards a different life—a life in touch with people and revolutionaries, with struggle, knowledge, art, the great ideals of the century, and the life of all mankind. Uspensky's break with the attitudes and psychology of his native environment and his embarking on a new life took place in difficult family and financial circumstances, and at a time

(1862-68) of complex social conditions. Uspensky spoke of the "hellish conditions" of life, of his "homelessness" in the first years after he struck out on his own. He experienced the wave of reaction which started in the early 1860's and which led to the suppression of *Sovremennik* and *Russkoe slovo* and the exile of Chernyshevsky; he grieved over the death of Dobrolyubov and witnessed the split among the intelligentsia (XIV, p. 211). Those were the years which Vasily A. Sleptsov described in his novel *Hard Times* (*Trudnoe vremya*); it was a time when the "good people" and "leading figures" began to disappear and Petersburg was deserted.

Uspensky lived through these years with courage. In this he was helped, while he was still in his teens and early youth, by his extreme sensitiveness to the sufferings of others, by his increasing disaffection with the corrupt surroundings in which he grew up, and finally, by good books, the youth circle in Chernigov, and his school life.

In his fight for a "new spiritual life" Uspensky received much encouragement from many kind and sympathetic friends. These included editors and writers for *Sovremennik* and especially for the lately rejuvenated *Otechestvennye zapiski* (*The Fatherland Notes*). Uspensky also found persons of like spirit among Russian revolutionaries-emigrants whom he came to know during his travels abroad in 1872 and 1875-76. In them Uspensky saw men who wanted to bring about great changes in Russia for the good of the people, men who "roamed abroad, constantly thinking about" their homeland, but at the same time "being constantly aware of the impossibility of living in it and working for it" ("Murder Will Out," a satirical sketch, VI, p. 45).

Uspensky also had moral support from revolutionaries living in Russia in the 1870's and 1880's. He was attracted to the progressive *raznochintsy* who were actively working underground and with determination. There are passages from his autobiographical writings indicating that Uspensky wrote for the revolutionary movement and derived inspiration from it. According to one of the Russian revolutionaries, Vera N. Figner, Uspensky was the best loved author of her generation, and his contacts with the revolutionaries "straightened him out."[7] And indeed it was so. To Uspensky, the Russian revolutionary was the embodiment of the best man. Uspensky knew many prominent members of the Populist movement, including German A. Lopatin, Vera Figner, Andrey I. Zhelyabov, Sofya L. Perovskaya, Yury N. Bogdanovich, Sergey M. Kravchinsky (Stepnyak), Alexander I. Ivanchin-Pisarev, and Dmitry A. Klements. Uspensky once thought of writing a novel—to be entitled *A Daring and Good Fellow*—based on the unusual life of Lopatin. In his writings, Uspensky expressed the feelings, convictions, and bitter disappointments of the revolutionaries of his time with deep understanding and sympathy, for those feelings, convictions and disappointments were his as well.

IV   A New Type of Writer

Uspensky's formative years coincided with a time of social and political turmoil in Russia, which fact explains the characteristic traits of Uspensky both as a man and a writer. In Uspensky, a new type of writer had emerged, one whose mission was to render selfless service to the Russian working people. This aim was embraced by Uspensky in his fight for spiritual regeneration, and it colored his entire moral and esthetic outlook. To progressive youth of the time Uspensky was a writer who wrote with "his heart's blood." Uspensky fought moral flabbiness, lack of will, and disparity between ideas and deeds. He hated the idea of tolerance of evil, calling instead for battle. For him it was not enough merely to write and to feel; one must express what one believed in deeds. In a letter to V. Sobolevsky, editor of *Russkie vedomosti* (*Russian Gazette*), written after a trip to Bulgaria in 1887 Uspensky proclaimed: "Yes! It is necessary *to act*, and to act *directly!*" As though speaking on behalf of progressives in Bulgaria, he continued:

Writer, do you have sympathy for this or that? Then prove it. Perhaps you will suffer for it? And badly? But for us that's not the question. We are not afraid to shoot scoundrels; we—your friends—who hate the scoundrels are not afraid to die. You must not be a coward, someone who is afraid of all this. If you writers write about this or that, then put it into practice. (XIV, p. 23)

The idea of proving one's convictions by deeds is found in many of Uspensky's works—"From the Notes of a Little Man" ("Iz zapisok malenkogo cheloveka"), "She Gave Her Life for the Course" ("Umerla za napravlenie"), "No Resurrection" ("Ne voskres").

Uspensky's works were closely linked to the poetic tradition of the Russian people with which he was thoroughly familiar. Uspensky collected folk tales and humorous and topical folk verses sung by factory workers; he often used folk songs, folk sayings, tales, and legends in his works, drawing mainly on the rich experience derived from his personal contacts with the people. He knew well the lives of artisans in Tula and in the villages of the Tula province, the peasants in the Samara region on the Volga who were often threatened with famine, and the peasants of the Novgorod region who toiled in severe climatic conditions. Uspensky made special studies of peasant migration, the sectarian movement, and the cooperatives formed by the people themselves. He visited Siberia where he met peasants who knew no masters or landlords and the Orenburg area which was shamelessly robbed by tsarist officials. He made trips to the agricultural South with its large farms; acquainted himself with the industrial Caucasus; turned his special attention to those parts of Russia where peasants ran away from their masters in search of a better life and the hardships which they subsequently encountered; and took a keen interest in the large-scale social disturbances in the south of Russia.

Uspensky carried on an extensive correspondence with working people belonging to various strata in Russian society.[8] He closely followed the press, especially provincial newspapers, brilliantly putting to use their material in his writings. In the Uspensky archives is a folder containing newspaper clippings for the years 1890-91 on the cover of which, written in Uspensky's handwriting are the words: (1) School, (2) Capital, (3) Migrants, (4) Peasant court and mob law. The folder also bears an inscription taken from Nekrasov's poem, "Reflections at the Main Entrance" ("Razmyshleniya u paradnogo vlcheda"), reflecting Uspensky's feelings about the material he had collected on the life of the people:

> Volga, Volga, when spring comes
> You do not flood the fields as much

As our land is now submerged
Under the great sufferings of our people.

Uspensky had great insight into the psychology of the masses and postreform economics in Russia. He was able to turn a vast amount of factual knowledge into vivid artistic images, scenes, and dialogues: statistical data, records, and documents became legitimate material for literature. He had the rare ability to say much in a few words, and to say it so powerfully that the reader felt persuaded to act and to change the life around him. In his "Talks About Trades" Gorky described the impact which a reading of Uspensky's works produced on him. Uspensky, said Gorky, "awakened in us a kind of special anxiety and real feeling." Gorky agreed with some of his contemporaries that "after reading the work of Gleb Uspensky one wishes to do something decisive."[9]

CHAPTER 2

The Disastrous Rasteryaeva Street

"There was no place here for honest and sensible happiness."[1]

I Sketches and Tales (1862-1872)

THE theme of Uspensky's sketches and tales of the first period (1862-1872) is the fate of people doomed to strenuous labor and poverty. The life of the "dark people," especially artisans and peasants, contrasted with that of the parasitic ruling classes was portrayed with great sensitivity. Uspensky was particularly discerning in showing the "worthlessness of the surroundings." He created unusual, paradoxical images, fantastic characters bordering on caricatures, and amusing situations. Their purpose, however, was not merely to entertain, but to reveal the life of the time, its ugliness and senselessness. For example, in "Day of Need and Boredom" (1865), the dull and meaningless provincial life is revealed through the portrayal of a "provincial young man," a typical product of a small provincial town. The hero is described as being "something between a matchmaker or gossiping old woman and a chatty newspaper column." He was a spreader of news and a "consoler," whose services were demanded by the bored inhabitants of the town.

The drowsy and torpid provincial existence drawing people "into the depth of its stinking mire" is a recurrent subject of Uspensky's early works, and the life described there was one of deceit and obsequiousness, mentally crippling and devoid of happiness.

A literary device characteristic of Uspensky may be found in his works of the 1860's, namely, the combination of humor and satire. For example, humorous descriptions of ignorant, ordinary people are combined with satire on the executors of the latest orders from above. In "Loafer" ("Lentyay") (1865)

Uspensky gave a truthful picture of the "great reforms," characterizing them as the epoch of "frolicsome, sentimental nonsense." Unlike most journalists of his time who adopted a cheerful tone and whitewashed conditions in the towns and countryside, Uspensky described with biting humor the "changes" brought about by the 1861 reform. He portrayed the participants in the reform as first having a "wild party" proclaiming: "Brothers! For God's sake, let's think about nothing," and then going to the tsarist authorities in the role of "peace mediators" between the peasants and the landowners. The merging of humor and satire is particularly notable and acquires deep social meaning in the sketches, *Fathers and Sons (Otsy i deti)* (1865).

The humorous and comic in Uspensky's works increasingly came to have tragic overtones towards the mid-1860's along with the development of more open and direct satire ("Misery Sings Its Songs," 1866). This transformation of humor into satire, the comic into the tragic, is closely linked to the tradition of Nikolay Gogol and his followers, notably Nikolay Saltykov-Shchedrin.

The goals of the democratic movement of the 1860's were to tell the truth about the people and to determine without fear the causes for the hard life of the people. These became the guiding principles for Uspensky throughout his creative life. He began to understand the conditions in which Russia developed after the 1861 reform and to realize that the old forces continued to hold back the new and that the habits and ways of the old (i.e., of the serf-owners) were carried over in implementing the reforms.

Uspensky's style in the 1860's can be clearly seen in his classical tale "Sentry Box" ("Budka") (1868), which was Uspensky's first contribution to the *Otechestvennye zapiski* edited by Nekrasov.

"Sentry Box" tells about an everyday, typical occurrence in the life of a Russian provincial town, about how an ordinary policeman on duty "ruled" the people.

The policeman, Mymretsov, who embodies the spirit of autocracy, is a frightening character. He is a man of "utter stupidity," in whom "nearly all human aspirations have been suppressed," and who has a "thirst for vodka" (III, p. 354). All traces of a human being have been destroyed in Mymretsov by military drills, but the fact that he is "mentally crippled" enables him successfully to perform his duties which consist either in dragging people away or "not letting them in." His whole life, in fact, becomes an act of "dragging" people away so that he "came to see in people only the back of their collar and differentiate people from animals and things by that object alone" (III, p. 356). Through this comic situation Uspensky revealed the tragic fate of the ordinary people who were often dragged away by the collar to the police station in the name of law and order.

Mymretsov, however, also had his problems: When he was not practicing the act of "dragging away" or "not letting in" people, he was bored. And his most difficult moments were caused by the appearance of some poor half-clad person who "didn't even have a real collar on the back of his neck" so that there was "nothing to grab him by." In such instances people would cry triumphantly, "There's nothing you can do!" (III, p. 370).

In "Sentry Box" Uspensky also described the victims of Mymretsov's practice, for "in every collar there is a whole drama" (III, p. 372). There was the frightened laundry woman fighting to be free from her "parasitic husband"; the alcoholic tailor, Danilka; the ever-hungry old beggar with his children; and the worker who jumped into a boiling kettle to avoid being recruited into the army. And all the time the sinister and illiterate Mymretsov was heard shouting: "Where's my stick?..." (III, p. 359).

To Mymretsov one may well apply the comment by Belinsky about the petty clerk, Ivan Antonovich, in Gogol's *Dead Souls*. Ivan Antonovich was an ordinary, insignificant clerk, and yet he possessed infinite power over the lives of people. Belinsky said:

Of course, some Ivan Antonovich with his juglike face is a very funny thing in a book by Gogol, and an insignificant phenomenon in life. But if you should have any dealing with him, you would quickly lose the wish to laugh at him, and you would not find him so insignificant after all. . . . Why should he appear so important to you in life—that is the question![2]

Gogol answered that question, and so did Uspensky, who
showed that Mymretsov, like Ivan Antonovich, was not at all
an accidental, petty, or even a funny phenomenon in life. In
him was embodied the evil force of autocracy. Like the keeper
of law and order in Chekhov's story, "Noncommissioned Officer
Prishibeev" ("Unter Prishibeev") Mymretsov is a stereotyped
character. In the revolutionary underground press of the 1870's
the character of Mymretsov with his practice of "dragging" and
"not letting in" people became the embodiment of the autocratic
regime in Russia.

II   Manners of Rasteryaeva Street

The ideas and style that took shape in Uspensky's sketches
and tales of the 1860's were fully developed in two most
important and related works by Uspensky of the same period:
Manners of Rasteryaeva Street and *Ruin* (*Razorenie*). In these
works the fatal influence on man of the ugly, everyday socio-
economic conditions was clearly shown.

Manners of Rasteryaeva Street (*Nravy Rasteryaevoy ulitsi*)
(1866) is a major work in which century-old customs and mores
of a Russian provincial town (chiefly Tula) of the early 1860's
are described. The life of the town is condensed into one main
idea: *rasteryaevshchina* (the state of being morally and spiritually lost). This state is accompanied by lethargy, fear of life
and of one's superiors and authorities, spiritual emptiness,
debased human relations, confusion, indifference to intellectual
and social questions, and perpetual poverty and sorrow. In
Gorky's view, "the social value of these books remains great for
our time; in general Uspensky's tales have not lost their educational significance."[3]

The distinctive traits of Uspensky as a writer can be most
clearly seen in *Manners of Rasteryaeva Street*: complete truthfulness and sincerity in portraying workers; a profound sense
of sorrow over their fate and, as Gorky noted, "extreme sensitivity ... anger and repulsion before a 'general state of dehumanization.' "[4] Uspensky was above all interested in showing how the
social and domestic life, and the moral codes of Rasteryaeva
Street formed the character of those living there, turning one
into a kulak (Prokhor), another into a torturer (Tolokonnikov)

who delighted in humiliating and beating those under him, a third into someone who regarded his degrading existence as happiness (Kapiton Ivanov), and a fourth into a quack (Khripushin).

On Rasteryaeva Street people became used to the inhuman conditions of their life and failed to notice its ugliness. And if someone like Prokhor would decide "to live like a human being," in whom a sense of human dignity was awakened, his energy, will, mind, and moral strength were used not "for the good of all," but rather for attaining personal wealth by "getting on the back of one's fellow man and being the boss...." Prokhor is a considerable achievement. Through him Uspensky revealed the rise of the earliest representatives of capitalism in Russia. The Prokhors were no strangers, no "foreigners"; they were not an accidental phenomenon, but grew out of Russian reality at that time.

In his works Uspensky showed different attitudes toward characters from different social strata. The humor of *Manners of Rasteryaeva Street* is sad and joyless, but a note of gentleness is present when the descriptions concern "little people"—the working class—among whom were skilled journeymen of dignity. Uspensky loved such people and felt sympathy towards them. With understanding and gentle humor he portrayed the tragedy of their lives: Talented persons became drunkards; pitifully confused, they cursed their fate and became accustomed to a life of servitude.

But Uspensky's humor became biting and ironic when he came to depict a character like Prokhor who chose to become a predator, yet a small, but vicious and strong beast. In comparing and contrasting the exploiters and tormentors on the one hand and their victims on the other, Uspensky unfolded a cheerless picture of the life and manners of Rasteryaeva Street. This is reflected in the style of the work in which there are no entertaining intrigues or plots. Like other *raznochintsy* Uspensky was a literary reformer, abandoning the literary canons of the time and creating new literary devices. In *Manners of Rasteryaeva Street* Uspensky for the first time used the device of linking a number of sketches and tales into one literary cycle.

Manners of Rasteryaeva Street is a cycle of sketches linked by a single theme. The sketches constitute a lively gallery of por-

traits whose subjects are in one way or another mentally crippled
and dehumanized. For example, Khripushin is a "medicine
man" whose physiognomy was one of the main reasons for his
success. "One has never seen," Uspensky writes, "a more
devastating face." Khripushin had a nose like a button, large
bulging cheeks, a fiery mustache that looked like a Turkish saber,
eyes glistening with a metallic sheen, and a head like a globe.
This absurd face, which recalls Gogol's caricatures and gives
the impression of a loaded gun, and Khripushin's quack medicine
are personifications of the muddle-headedness, senselessness,
ignorance, and barbarism which characterized Rasteryaeva
Street.

The psychology which Rasteryaeva Street produced was that
of the helpless slave, the revengeful tormentor, or the parasitic
kulak. With insight and understanding Uspensky created Tolokonnikov, a character who reflects the psychology of a slave—
which contained within it elements of the psychology of a
tormentor—against which he would struggle all his life.

In Russia, Rasteryaeva Street has long been regarded as the
embodiment of Philistinism in the country and of the horrors
of the inhuman life which Uspensky experienced personally.
Rasteryaeva Street turned people into frightened, ignorant
beings, who were in a constant state of fear. "One must always
be afraid—this is life's basic truth"—such was the philosophy of
the people residing on Rasteryaeva Street.[5]

This philosophy of life was also well known to Gorky who,
like Uspensky, came from the heart of the petty bourgeois world.
But Gorky, in portraying the everyday life of this world, used
different artistic methods and showed a different outlook on
life in *The City of Okurov* (*Gorodok Okurov*), *Life of Matvey
Kozhemyakin* (*Zhizn' Matveya Kozhemyakina*), *Childhood*
(*Detstvo*), *Into the World* (*Vlyudyakh*), *My Universities* (*Moi
universitety*). Uspensky dreamed of liberating Rasteryaeva Street
and joining it to the larger world; he dreamed that hopes and
desires, the "angel of awakened conscience" would one day
appear on Rasteryaeva Street; but "not a single spark of hope
can be seen" on that dead street. Uspensky in the 1860's did not
know what forces would finally destroy that fatal power which
the petty bourgeois world exercised over the minds, life, and the
behavior of Russian people. Thus, the prevailing tone of

Manners of Rasteryaeva Street is one of depression, pain, melancholy, and bitterness. The sad humor of the work is akin to a tragic sense of doom. In the works by Gorky, on the other hand, scenes and characters are set against the background of such events as the Russo-Japanese war and the 1905 Russian Revolution. These events shook the ground from under the petty bourgeois world. Thus, even in tragic scenes there is a sense of anticipation of radical social changes.

III Ruin

In 1869 in *Otechestvennye zapiski* appeared Uspensky's second important work, *Ruin—Observations of Mikhail Ivanovich* (*Razorenie—Nablyudeniya Mikhaila Ivanovicha*). In 1871 it was published in book form in St. Petersburg. Later, in Uspensky's first collected works (1883) it became part of a trilogy entitled *Ruin* (*Sketches of Provincial Life*), the two other works being *Meek and Mild* (*Tishe vody, nizhe travy*) (1870) and *Observations of a Lazy Man* (*Nablyudeniya odnogo lentyayá*) (1871).

The theme of the trilogy is the ruin of those whose well-being was based on slavery and oppression and who lost their source of income as a result of the social and economic changes following the abolition of serfdom. The ruin was not only material; it marked a crisis in the old outlook on life, the collapse of traditional family relations and social conventions. The old way of life based on serfdom gave way to new ideas and attitudes.

In manner and tone *Ruin* considerably differs from *Manners of Rasteryaeva Street;* the differences indicate greater artistic mastery on the part of Uspensky, greater maturity of outlook, and a more critical approach to social questions. *Ruin* marks a turning point in Uspensky's literary output, for in ideas and style it goes back to his preceding works, especially the first part of the trilogy, and anticipates his works of the 1870's and 1880's.

In portraying the bitter life of ruthlessly exploited people in the postreform period, Uspensky not only noted "all kinds of mental and moral cripplement" and the distortion of human aspirations, but also showed how his heroes were tormented by the life around them, and how the people began to sense

the futility of their surroundings and yearned for a different
life. All this is brilliantly described in *Ruin,* especially through
the character of the worker from Tula, Mikhail Ivanovich. Here
Uspensky turned from the apathy and oppressiveness of Rasteryaeva Street to an active search for answers to problems, to the
"clearing up" of the mind, and to the birth of "new, undefined
strivings among the masses" (III, p. 8). Uspensky had praise
for those who labored, and spoke of work with deep respect,
contrasting it to the "oppressive emptiness of inaction." In
Uspensky's view labor was the great healer and savior of man,
rescuing him from humiliation and moral degradation. The
major theme of Uspensky's works of the 1860's—contrast between
those who labored and those who practiced various forms of
parasitism—is powerfully dealt with in *Ruin.*

In this work Uspensky portrayed a number of workers who
begin to be sharply aware of the gap between their pitiful
existence and a life of purpose and dignity. They try to understand the causes of this intolerable gap and even to find means
of eliminating it. As a contrast to the world of apathy and sub-
missiveness, Uspensky created the worker-rebel, Mikhail Ivanovich, who was also part of the Rasteryaeva world, but with an
awakened social conscience. His thoughts were not concerned
with *achieving* personal material security (as in the case of
Prokhor in *Manners of Rasteryaeva Street*), but with the need
for *improving* the lives of all working people. Mikhail Ivanovich
spoke not only about the right of the working people to have
bread, but thought about their need for spiritual nourishment.
He was convinced that power was on the side of those who
labored, and therefore, condemned the existing, unjust social
system.

The new tasks that Uspensky set for himself in *Ruin* called
for new artistic devices. In terms of composition, *Manners of
Rasteryaeva Street* may be regarded as a lively gallery of por-
traits; portrait-painting turned out to be an effective means of
typifying the dull, empty life of Rasteryaeva Street. In *Ruin,*
Uspensky's main task was not to show how people of the Rasteryaeva type were formed, but how the masses, oppressed and
intellectually backward, began to question things and groped
for answers to their problems. Thus, what is most important
about *Ruin* is not the portrayal of characters and everyday life,

but descriptions of inner feelings, strivings and hopes, clashes
and conflicts. This is clearly shown in the frank, impassioned,
and stirring speeches of Mikhail Ivanovich. The ruinous surroundings and the resultant dehumanization are seen through
the eyes of an enlightened worker. The soul of Mikhail Ivanovich,
embittered by oppression, "could have no rest." All that had
been accumulated in his suffering heart "burst forth and gushed
out like a river"; "he had to speak, to speak out"; he "seeks
those who would listen to him"; "everywhere one can hear him,
who is suffering from consumption." Words and phrases taken
from his speeches give a picture of human relations existing in
that absurd, unjust world: "robber"; "to turn ordinary folks into
blockheads"; "oppressor"; "people with full bellies strolling
about"; "others have eaten our bread"; "expelled for rebellion,
disobedience, because I would not let them rob"; "a system
based on robbery." Mikhail Ivanovich spoke about the rights of
the working man to lead a human, dignified life. "It is time,"
he said, "to let the ordinary man have some breathing space! . . .
Give him a way! . . ." (III, p. 12).

The character of the "rebel" gunsmith, Mikhail Ivanovich,
who was dismissed from the munitions factory for throwing a
stone at a leaseholder of the factory, was not a mere artistic
invention having no roots in the national soil. The character was
based on life in Russia in the 1860's when the workers' movement
began to emerge, a movement which involved the munitions
factory in Tula. Through the character of Mikhail Ivanovich,
Uspensky expressed both hatred against the existing order of
life and a yearning for the liberation of millions of people
oppressed by serfdom.

In *Ruin* the peasant also speaks out. The hero of the second
part of the trilogy, *Meek and Mild,* is the peasant miller, Ivan
Nikolaevich. Ivan Nikolaevich believes that the peasant cannot
find truth anywhere. His dream is to get into the local agricultural administration which he hopes will enable him to protect
the peasant fom hunger and ruin, from ignorance and deceit
(III, p. 233).

Talking with a "clever peasant" was the accusation made
against Mikhail Ivanovich in the first part of the trilogy and
marks the significant moment in the second part. The second
part is in the form of a diary kept by Vasily Petrovich, a

raznochinets. Vasily Petrovich had "in his life known many fainthearted persons ... wavering, lacking the courage of their convictions." He himself is insufficiently firm in his belief and is shattered by difficulties presented by life. Thus, he feels a sense of relief when he talks with the strong and determined Ivan Nikolaevich, through whose eyes he sees the miserable life in the village. He is drawn toward the peasant in the same way that Nadya Cheremukhina and Sofya Ptitsyna, helpless and thirsting for a new life, were drawn to Mikhail Ivanovich in the first part of *Ruin.*

Uspensky describes various forms of awakening of the working people and their search for answers to the urgent questions facing them. For example, he tells about the peasants' community-sect, whose members in their prayer sought their defenders "in heaven" while carrying out their idea of peasant "communism" on earth. "Everything that we produce will be equally divided among us," they said, and as a result they had warm sheepskins and enough food (*Meek and Mild*).

In *Ruin,* besides the workers, Uspensky portrayed various types of intellectuals and made frequent comparisons—directly or indirectly—between Mikhail Ivanovich and Ivan Nikolaevich on the one hand, and on the other hand, the passive, contemplative intellectuals who had goodness in their hearts, but were resigned or decadent: Vasily Cheremukhin, Utkin, Vanyushka, Ermakov, and others. Uspensky looked at these weak-willed intellectuals from two points of view: the urgent demands of the awakened working people and the ideas held by those socially and politically conscious representatives of the toiling masses who were able to make open and resolute protests. These comparisons led to the author's conclusion that the intellectuals—including the best educated ones who secretly discussed the Paris Commune, or others, like the clerk Zmeev who went to ridiculous lengths "in order to prove that he is a human being,"—were unable to answer the questions asked by the awakened masses. And they were unable really to rebel against the existing order or to be inspired by ideas showing the way to a new life.

These intellectuals belonged to that split generation which had been brilliantly characterized by the critic, Nikolay A.

Dobrolyubov. In his article, "When Will the Real Day Come?" ("Kogda zhe pridyot nastoyashehy den'?") he wrote:

These people know where the root of evil lies and know what must be done to put an end to evil; they are deeply and genuinely imbued with the idea which they finally attained. But they no longer have the strength for practical activity; they have so strained themselves that their character somehow became enfeebled. They welcome the approach of the new life, but they cannot go out to meet it, and are unable to respond to and satisfy the fresh feeling experienced by the man who is thirsting to do good and looking for a leader.[6]

These words well describe the situation with which Uspensky dealt in his work. The "fresh feeling" of the worker, Mikhail Ivanovich, could not be satisfied by those "who want to act, but cannot." Uspensky's worker wished "to do good" and searched for a real teacher, but Cheremukhin could not be that teacher, for he lacked the strength to fight, and to carry out practical deeds.

Another aspect of the portrayal of Mikhail Ivanovich is the originality of Uspensky's treatment in terms of idea-content and style. Uspensky showed the loneliness of his hero who found few listeners among the Tula working people, and Mikhail Ivanovich more than once landed in comic situations. In impassioned moments he, for lack of listeners, had to "seek assistance in inanimate objects" (III, p. 12). The "awakening," the anticipation of "freedom," the acknowledgement that "oppression" had not yet reached the intolerable stage, ridicule, and the absence of sympathetic and understanding listeners all made Mikhail Ivanovich feel completely alone and abandoned. Uspensky spoke of his "fallen spirit," "sick and beaten head," and "sick soul." Thus, the comic situation of the worker had tragic overtones. This situation was—in a way—funny, but it only testified, objectively, to the over-all tragic situation and to the fact that the working masses were still far from realizing wherein lay their interests. However, the very fact that workers like Mikhail Ivanovich appeared on the scene forewarned of an approaching crisis for the old order and the imminent awakening of the working masses.

There is yet another tragic aspect to Uspensky's trilogy. Here reality is portrayed from the angle of what the people were hoping for, what they expected from "liberty," and what they actually got. The people dreamed of being able to breathe freely; they awaited liberation as the day of the "coming of the Messiah." Such fond expectations were also shared by the worker-dreamer, Mikhail Ivanovich. But they turned out to be mirages. What the people were waiting for did not come about. Uspensky saw this clearly, but his beloved hero failed to analyze and understand it and once again fell into a comic situation. Uspensky made fun of his hero's illusory "blissful moments," putting him into a situation which revealed the glaring disparity between the fervent desires of the people who "made their mouths water" by talking about "freedom" and the pitifully small possibilities they had in realizing their desires. All they could do was to be content with the fact that they had the right to freedom, if not the means of exercising it.

For example, Mikhail Ivanovich felt that he had scored an important victory when he managed to eat in the railway dining car together with gentlemen. In this, Uspensky again showed the comedy of Mikhail Ivanovich's campaign for freedom. In creating such scenes, Uspensky revealed the essence of the epoch of the "great reforms" which had aroused such sweet anticipations and happy hopes, and then buried them. The people received little from the authorities besides words of regret. This explains the sorrow and bitterness with which Uspensky described the dreams of his hero, his anticipations of a new life, and his triumphant journey to St. Petersburg—complete with sugared cakes!

The over-all picture of life painted by Uspensky was a dismal and suffocating one. This impression is all the stronger since *Ruin*, like many works by other democrat-writers of the 1860's, was left unfinished. This incomplete state of the trilogy suggests that the author himself did not know where to lead his restless hero-dreamer in search of a better life.

Gleb Uspensky in the 1860's was one of the outstanding members of the group of *raznochintsy* writers which included Nikolay V. Uspensky, Fyodor M. Reshetnikov, Nikolay G. Pomyalovsky, Vasily A. Sleptsov, and Alexander I. Levitov. These men were united by common artistic principles and spiritual strivings, and their works show a similar understanding of Russian reality. In their works the material and spiritual existence of man is shown as depending on certain factors in life to which Russian literature of the first half of the nineteenth century had paid little or no attention. They reveal a new conception of environment related to new social conditions, and to the ideological and philosophical search of the 1860's. They discovered a most important factor in life—economic relations—and depicted the first clashes between conflicting economic interests in Russia after the abolition of serfdom.

These democrats and writers of the 1860's regarded social and economic life from the point of view of the interests, situation, and fate of the working masses. The subject of their works were the joys and sorrows of the ordinary people. In their opinion, the most important thing was to go to the people, to become educated by sharing the people's work, sufferings, and happiness, and make the people's interests their own. Labor, especially physical labor of the people, was the most significant element in life as they portrayed it. To them, the moral content of a man's life, the education of his children, and his own development as an individual depended on his attitude toward labor. In *Manners of Rasteryaeva Street,* Uspensky showed that the source of all the unhappiness of the Preterpeev sisters lay in the fact that they did not understand the meaning of labor and looked upon it as something degrading. Their wrong attitude toward labor deprived them of the only reliable means of defense from their tormentor, Tolokonnikov.

These plebeian writers of the 1860's also enriched Realism by their treatment of characters. They revealed the tragic dependence of man on circumstances, showing how social reality of the time was opposed to human feelings and aspirations, and that it did not nourish human capacities but destroyed them. In this respect *Manners of Rasteryaeva Street* deserves to be placed next to Nikolay G. Pomyalovsky's *Seminary Sketches (Ocherki bursy)*. In various forms and with various degrees of depth these writers showed, in Uspensky's words, the "frustration and stifling of human demands." At the same time, however, Uspensky, Pomyalovsky, Fyodor M. Reshetnikov, and Sleptsov did not ascribe any fatal quality to the influence of circumstance on man. They showed how man could resist circumstance. This struggle against circumstance represented an important victory for Realism, and it had great significance in the portrayal of representatives of the working class, for it showed how a passive unthinking attitude toward life was replaced by a questioning, thinking, and an active attitude towards reality by resistance against oppressive surroundings.

CHAPTER 3

Western Europe and Russia
as Seen by Uspensky

"Terrible, but clear and understandable."

I Impressions Abroad

THE year 1873 marked the beginning of a new period in Uspensky's life and literary career. In 1872 and 1875-76 Uspensky visited several Western European countries. His impressions of those countries and the part they played in shaping his views—as reflected in his literary works—have been included in his *Autobiography*. "My personal biography," he said, "up to about 1871 should definitely be ignored; all of it was one continuous problem—the difficulty 'of living and thinking,' and it took much time and energy to be freed of it finally" (XIV, p. 580).

Speaking about his spiritual rebirth in the *Autobiography*, Uspensky recounted those developments he observed abroad which had had an influence on the shaping of his new life. The most important among them was the Paris Commune. Uspensky arrived in Paris several months after the fall of the Commune and witnessed the executions of the Communards. His anger against the "evildoers"—those who strangled the Commune—and his deep compassion for the Communards were preserved forever in his "spiritual genealogy" and were reflected in his works of the 1870's and 1880's. To Uspensky, the Paris Commune was an event resulting from the entire social make-up of Western Europe. It helped him understand that bitter struggle against irreconcilable enemies was the only law possible in a bourgeois society. It also showed him that the working masses had realized the intolerableness of the life they led, and that the struggle between the oppressed and the oppressor would continue.

In his "book of spiritual genealogy" Uspensky recorded his unforgettable impressions of the Louvre. He also described his journey to London, where he met Pyotr L. Lavrov—one of the leaders of the Russian revolutionary Populists living abroad—and came to know a more highly developed capitalist society. It was about this aspect of London life that he wrote in some of his works ("There They Know"). The "crowdedness of London" was an image repeatedly used by Uspensky in describing social relations in a capitalist society. In the river that was London the "pike eats the carp...."

Finally, Uspensky in his *Autobiography* spoke about his journey to Serbia ("straight from Paris") which had recently risen in revolt against Turkish rule. The importance of this trip (taken in October-December, 1876) was fully described in his "Letter from Serbia ("Pisma iz Serbii") (1876-77) and "No Resurrection" ("Ne Voskres") (1877). In the censored editions, Uspensky could not speak about the colonial policy of the Russian government, though he thoroughly understood the dark, mercenary machinations of the "great liberators." This, however, did not prevent him from recognizing the positive role played by those Russians who took part in the national liberation movement in the Balkans. A number of Russian revolutionaries went to Serbia as volunteers.

The events in Serbia once again convinced him that the people in Russia must carry out radical changes in their lives. Like his friends from among the revolutionaries, Uspensky hoped that the social upheaval that had taken place as a result of the national liberation movement of the Slavs would be the beginning of the struggle for democratic changes in Russia. In "No Resurrection," the painful scene of the return of the Serbian boy to his master from whom he had earlier run away opened the eyes of Dolbezhnikov to the inhuman social relations existing not only among the Serbs, but also in Russia. The need to liberate the Serbian boy made Dolbezhnikov aware of the larger task to be accomplished in Russia. "The boy," said Dolbezhnikov, "has destroyed my peace, my health—everything, in the space of a second.... The thought that something else is now needed was for me absolutely clear" (IV, p. 241).

One should not, however, consider Uspensky's impressions and reflections abroad merely in terms of the changes that occurred in his work and outlook. In order to understand Uspensky's development from 1873 on, it is necessary to look into those ideas and thoughts expressed in his works written before that year.

In summing up the significance of what he had observed abroad, Uspensky wrote in his *Autobiography*: "I had written little about this, but I have learned much from it and have jotted down, once and for all, much that is good in my book of spiritual genealogy" (IV, p. 579).

When Uspensky went abroad he was a convinced democrat, though not yet a Socialist. He carried with him on his trips thoughts about the people of Russia and about the beginnings of their awakening. He invariably spoke about his impressions and observations abroad from one point of view: the comparison of life in the West and in Russia.

II *New Artistic Manner*: Sick Conscience

In the 1870's Uspensky created a new type of literary work, whose characteristic features were fully developed in *Sick Conscience* (*Bolnaya sovest'*) (1873). Uspensky's artistic thinking in the 1860's had fallen within the limits of the usual, traditional literary genres. *Ruin* was considered by Uspensky both as a novel and a tale. At that time he felt no particular need for creating new forms of existing genres and artistic methods. Basically, his works belonged to the type of sketches written by democratic, plebeian writers of the 1850's, such as *Provincial Sketches* (*Gubernskie ocherki*) by Nikolay Saltykov-Shchedrin, and they occupied an important place in the literary movement of the 1860's. To be sure, *Manners of Rasteryaeva Street* and especially *Ruin* had considerably outgrown the forms of sketch-literature of the 1850's and 1860's, but they were nonetheless closely linked in terms of methods of artistic representation.[1]

By the 1870's Uspensky had become acutely aware of the impossibility of continuing his work in the old manner. He turned aside from the traditional genres which did not serve his purpose and sought instead semi-imaginative, semi-journalistic forms which could—in his opinion—dramatically and sharply convey the sense of growing instability and contradiction of Russian life during the transitional period. He wanted these forms to make it possible for him to respond quickly to the issues of the day and at the same time enable him fully to express his own anxiety over the condition and fate of the common man in Russia. In creating this new type of semi-imaginative, semi-journalistic narrative, Uspensky also wished to involve the reader in the process of his observation and thinking.

With this original imaginative-journalistic genre, Uspensky was consciously responding to the demands arising from the life of the Russian people. He understood—and this can be seen already in *Ruin*—that working people needed to be led to the light, and have explained to them where real truth was to be found and what constituted true happiness. The intelligentsia, whose duty was to work for the people, expected powerful, sincere, and heartfelt words from literature that would rouse them and inspire them to serve the people, and to perform heroic deeds. It followed that the artist had to be in close relation with his reader; he had to "untie his own hands" and create the narrative forms that would give him the greatest freedom.

In a letter of 1875 written from Paris to his friend, Antony Kamensky, Uspensky described his new style, linking it .to the tasks of the time:

I decided to put all that I am thinking about and what I have in my head at present into some order and write in the forms in which my thoughts come to me, without resorting to the existing forms of the tale and the sketch which are extremely restricting. There will be sketches and scenes and reflections, placed in some sort of order, that is, arranged in such a way that the reader would understand, for example, why this sketch follows that scene. (XIII, p. 156)

This may be considered Uspensky's manifesto, and Uspensky brilliantly fulfilled the program he had set for himself. In creating an original type of semi-imaginative, semi-journalistic literature Uspensky enriched Russian classical literature.

Uspensky's first work in the new style is *Sick Conscience,* which astounded contemporary readers by its unusualness and its sharp departure from his preceding works. The work did not lend itself easily to classification according to traditional genres. Critics called it a "sketch," but the term is inaccurate in describing the work, for it tends to obscure the new artistic principles underlying it, principles about which Uspensky wrote in his letter to Kamensky.

Probably the most important and distinguishing feature of *Sick Conscience* is its confessional, lyrical nature. The character of the author-narrator serves as the organizing center of the work. This device represents a prominent feature of Uspensky's works of the 1870's and 1880's. But *Sick Conscience* is not only a lyrical work. It also has an epic element which is seen in the imaginative re-creation of reality. This depiction omits petty, minute details of everyday life and psychology—characteristic of Uspensky's works of the 1860's. It is, instead, of a generalizing, sociological nature, and is combined with an analytical examination of life.

Contemporary readers also noted another characteristic of Uspensky's new works. The artistic method used in *Sick Conscience* was defined by some as *"a mixture of the imaginative and the journalistic."* The journalistic aspect can also be found in some of Uspensky's works of the 1860's, but there it is not yet organically united with the imaginative in forming a new type of literary work. This unity is found only in Uspensky's works of the 1870's in which the imaginative acquires features of journalistic exposure and singleness of purpose, while the journalistic is enriched by the imaginative approach.

Sick Conscience consists of a series of miniature journalistic sketches, fictitious scenes, and sociological and moral reflections. They are united, not by images and subject matter, but by problems. After giving a brief, satirical, and vivid sketch of the pompousness and complacency of the German military establishment which had crushed France in 1871, Uspensky concludes with the refrain: "No, we don't have such things any more"; "No, things are better with us." Then, as a contrast, he reproduces a short conversation with Kudinych, a Russian soldier ("a good soul") which leads him to the same conclusion: "No, things are better with us!" Referring to the good roads in Europe, the author-narrator next takes the reader to Belgium.

He draws a sketch of Belgium's industrial hell and points to the strained relationship between the owners and the workers. Then, as a contrast—as in the first case—he portrays a short scene showing the patriarchal customs of Russian industrial enterprises. Again he concludes: "No, things are better with us!"

Turning to Paris he describes a military trial at Versailles and reaches the same conclusion but with an important additional comment: "I was convinced that they [the Versailles courts] were really evil, and their doings are evil because they are evil." The Russian courts and public procurators are different: They

have no malice towards the peasant, for example, who cut down a tree and must be put in jail for it; as a matter of fact, they feel sorry for the peasant. They have learned to love the people, and if sometimes they send him to Siberia they do it as a matter of duty, but *personally* they even pity him and give him money.... (IV, pp. 339-40)

The second chapter of *Sick Conscience* begins with a statement of the thesis that in Western Europe private convictions and public actions were in harmony with one another. "Thus," Uspensky wrote, "what the unjust Versailles courts and the Berlin beasts (German soldiers) do is only what personal moral needs lead them to do." To illustrate and prove this thesis Uspensky returns to the contrasts described in the first chapter. There the contrasts reveal certain phenomena in life, but unaccompanied by analysis or comments by the author (except for the last quotation given above about the courts). In the second chapter the contrasts are treated analytically and with a sociological emphasis, notably from the point of view of the condition of the workingman and the prospects of his liberation.

Returning to the comparison of Belgian and Russian industrial enterprises, Uspensky reached an important conclusion: "Bent with his head to the earth," he wrote, "the foreign worker knows who bent him; . . . he lives with anger and hatred which sooner or later will unbend him" (IV, p. 342). The situation of the Russian worker, Andron, was different. The shop steward cheated him, but the owner of the factory gave him five rubles. He got drunk on it for two weeks, and when he got sober again he "could not, for the life of him, decide who was at fault: he—Andron, Kuprianov [the shop steward], or the master..." When he found out that the master had done him a "good deed," "his thoughts got confused to the extent that he felt himself a fool" and was even grateful to the shop steward who had "straightened" him out by slapping him in the face and fining him for being absent from work. "I was a fool"—and with this thought Andron went back to work. Thus, in the second chapter Uspensky treated analytically the contrasts introduced in the first chapter, but in each case he reached the same conclusion.

Uspensky spoke about the definite, clear-cut social relations that existed in Western European countries and pointed to the absence of such relations in Russia. He was aware that the "reality" of such a distinct situation in Western Europe was deplorable: "The real attempt to believe only in the penny, the real moral decadence, the real endless poverty. . . ." But Uspensky did not merely condemn or express sorrow. In the "abominable situation" he tried to find something "instructive" and "not abominable." He saw that these distinct social relations in Western Europe were leading to the birth of a force capable someday of destroying that truth which turned some into exploiters and killers while dooming others to hunger and ignorance, poverty and death. This grim and naked truth of bitter egoism which prevailed in Western Europe was good in that it created "phenomena that are considered great." These phenomena educated and hardened man in certain feelings, actions, and convictions and made the workers rise and fight.

In Russia, on the other hand,

I came to meet Communards who might be content with the philosophy of the silver penny, retrogrades who believe deep down in their souls that they ought to be liberals, and liberals who, perhaps, as a matter of fact, are not liberals. . . . The whole thing, in a word, is something neither yes nor no, neither this nor that, neither going nor coming. . . . (IV, p. 357)

The fifth and concluding chapter of *Sick Conscience* deals with this phenomenon of "neither yes or no." He tells of the godless peasant who observed church rites; the spy who despised what he was doing, but was persuaded that "it would be better if this foul . . . business were in the hands of an honest man"; the "indecisive" monk who was preparing to take monastic vows and at the same time tried to get a job on the railway.

A general picture of the "abnormal spirit" was shown through the character of Ivan Nikolaevich who "piled up on himself various directions" which, however, "did not hold together in him." The reason was that Ivan Nikolaevich did everything (playing the liberal, falling in love) without conviction—but on someone else's order or suggestion—automatically, in conformity with what others were doing or were attracted to. The story of Ivan Nikolaevich appeared in *Otechestvennye zapiski* and was not included in Uspensky's collected works. But it is of basic importance to the entire work (*Sick Conscience*), for in it Uspensky gave his opinions on the whole phenomenon of "neither this nor that."

In portraying the depersonalized actions of Ivan Nikolaevich, Uspensky also revealed their social origins. Anticipating his sketches, "Paramon the Simpleton" ("Paramon Yurodivy") (1877), "Three Letters" ("Tri pisma") (1878), and *Willy-Nilly* (*Voley-nevoley*) (1884), Uspensky spoke about the general conditions of Russian life which deprived the common people of all possibilities of "exercising convictions." Ivan Nikolaevich was formed in an atmosphere in which people lived without convictions and were accustomed only to obey, cultivating the "logic of impotence." The inhabitants of Rasteryaeva Street obeyed the police, but their enlightened descendant, Ivan Nikolaevich came to obey literary fads. But even what he professed—under the influence of current fashions or suggestions from others—was not his own.

In suggesting that Russia was full of people with a "sick conscience" whose actions were based on the principle of "neither yes or no," Uspensky could be reproached for being somewhat one-sided, since, for example, there were factory owners who were quite capable—without any pangs of conscience —of bending the worker into a bow. He knew not only persons with a "sick conscience" but also those who were cruel, heartless, and willful executors of plans demanded by "order." He knew people whose conscience was perfectly healthy, clean, and free of every doubt and vacillation. They knew what they wanted; they thought and acted only in preserving their little nests, without being distracted by any consideration that was alien to their purpose. These types were described in the third chapter of *Sick Conscience*. Their way of life, Uspensky admitted, departed from the general rules and disproved his thesis about the "sickness and griefs of the abnormal spirit" in Russia (IV, p. 348).

But this is no contradiction. Uspensky did not at all intend to fit the different modes of life of his countrymen into one type characterized by a "sick conscience." The exceptions portrayed in the third chapter only confirmed his thought that the prevailing characteristic of the behavior of the Russian people was "neither this nor that."

The contrast between the "sick conscience" of the "pious atheists," "nonliberal liberals," and "nonvillainous villains" in Russia and the "truth of phenomena" in Western Europe makes clearer the meaning of the theme of the first chapter in *Sick Conscience*, "Things are better at home" (... U nas luchshe)— not at all because in Russia there were meek soldiers like Kudinych—who strongly resemble Tolstoy's Karataev—the development of whose personal qualities stopped at the "level of a ten-year-old"; or patriarchal-minded shop stewards like Kupriyanov; or factory owners like Fedoseev, who regarded with loathing profits earned by his own factory; or judges like Petrov, who sent the peasant to Siberia and at the same time felt sorry for him. Such formless individuals and their inconsistent actions bewildered and exasperated Uspensky who considered them manifestations of the patriarchal-Rasteryaeva way-of-life: lack of education, mental flabbiness, and absence of self-esteem and of properly developed social relations.

In the fourth chapter of *Sick Conscience* Uspensky speaks about the reason that made him yearn for home. "I wanted to leave," he said,

not because I was fed up with "truth"... I felt the need to leave just because I was afraid to lose this good impression of the truth of phenomena, for the phenomena themselves—the heart of the matter, the "berries" of the order of things existing in the world— are sometimes extremely unattractive, and here all the more so because they are "real." (IV, p. 354)

Thus, Uspensky differentiated the truth of phenomena (which he liked) from the phenomena themselves (which repelled him).

At the very beginning of the sketch Uspensky made one point clear: if he were to judge what he saw in Western Europe from the point of view of the order of things and from the point of view of one who wished to find the system there "even just a little newer," then "everything was worse there than with us...."

This idea, however, was not developed. The question as to why, from the point of view of the order of things, "things were better with us" was not answered by Uspensky who set himself other tasks. Nevertheless, the statement that "everything was worse there" was extremely important in terms of the further development of Uspensky's outlook and works.

Two years later in his sketch "There They Know" (1875) Uspensky, who had by then made his second trip abroad, answered the question that was left unanswered in *Sick Conscience*. In "There They Know" he repeated the basic idea of *Sick Conscience* using the same imaginative-journalistic form (with contrasts of life in Western Europe and Russia and a direct statement of his attitude towards them). He also pointed out the utter clarity and definiteness—the truthfulness of West European life, contrasting it with facts about Russia and its order of things, whose root causes were, so Uspensky thought, impossible to understand. These facts about Russian life depressed Uspensky.

The contrasts drawn in "There They Know" led Uspensky to the same conclusion about Western Europe as in *Sick Conscience*: "Terrible, but clear and understandable." But there was a new note: against the cruel and terrible truth, Uspensky saw the possibility of a different way of life which he sought for the Russian peasantry. "Standing on the deck," he wrote,

listening to the sound of waves, I thought about what I saw, and though I was deeply glad of what I saw, as I would of everything that is simple and genuine, I felt that this simplicity, this naked truth of the struggle for existence is terrible in its nakedness; that with us, on Russian soil, the struggle is not so merciless, that . . . there are people who like to act, not alone by themselves, but "all together": to be whipped all together, to have their homes burned all together, to go hungry all together. . . . Here I also recalled this condition: that it is still relatively unknown that a kind of real strength lies hidden somewhere, namely, in the poor Russian hut that does not even have a chimney for its fireplace, where people laugh and make jokes at meals made up only of cucumbers; or in mansions out of which people run seeking escape from their way of life and sometimes even envy the peasant. . . . These I recalled with special pleasure after what I saw, and I was glad to come home again. . . . (VI, pp. 15-16)

Uspensky introduced the idea of Russian village communal life, but he had no illusions about this life. He strictly delineated the *possibility* from the *reality* of Russian village life. It embittered him to see that the peasants who did things "not alone by themselves" had not yet done anything "all together" in the matter of improving their own lives. He pointed to the development of capitalism in the Russian village, to the destruction of the spirit of togetherness, and the appearance of peasant egoism —a sense of personal possession and alienation from common interests. Considering the objective socio-economic relations in Russia and abroad, Uspensky saw that the development of capitalism in Russia was, indeed, a fact. In 1875-76, on the basis of his observations abroad and knowledge of capitalist development at home, Uspensky wrote a number of socially penetrating works about the advance of capital in Russia, among them, "Bad News" and "Checkbook" ("Knizhka chekov").

In these works Uspensky showed the inhumanity of the new masters of Russia. At the same time, however, Uspensky recognized those progressive and positive aspects which capitalism had brought to Russia. In addition to the new type of factory owner, Myasnikov, and his horrible checkbook (in the sketch "Checkbook") which absorbed the country's natural wealth and the labor, blood, and life of people, there was also something new which destroyed the stagnant patriarch-serf relations, awakened the consciousness of the working people, and forced them "to think about everything."

The awakening consciousness of the workers under capitalist conditions is an important theme of the story, "Bad News." The story is about the beginning of a new life for a starved, stupefied, and muddle-headed beggar living in the village of Pokrovsky. The construction of a railway and the presence of new masters "gave work and money to an incalculable number of half-starved people...." The appearance of Pokrovsky and its inhabitants changed completely. Uspensky paid special attention—at this turning point in the life of the Russian village—to the spiritual rebirth of its culturally backward inhabitants. Capital and its new way of life liberated many people from the bonds of serfdom. "Mr. Dividend"—Uspensky's name for the capitalism which supplanted serfdom in Russia—annihilated century-old apathy and inaction. The new system of wage labor—"get your pay and get out"—gave the people a certain amount of material well-being; one could at least have three hours every day that were free from work. And with leisure came thought, the need to think—"the next unwelcomed guest, after money, of those god-forsaken places." The right to think about oneself and about one's situation, was, in Uspensky's view, a great thing for the millions of people brought up in ways that had existed for centuries characterized by exhausting labor and actions in accordance with someone else's thoughts and orders.

The development of capitalism in Russia exposed the con-flicting interests of people; it caused their behavior and convic-tions to become better defined, destroying the source of the "sick conscience" and eliminating the possibility of acting and thinking according to the principle of "neither yes nor no." Ivan Kuzmich Myasnikov in "Checkbook" had nothing in common with the factory owner Fedoseev in *Sick Conscience*. Myasnikov had definite plans in life, and he thought and acted strictly according with these plans. A "sick conscience" did not exist for him. Uspensky, however, did not go further in developing his thoughts about the positive effects of nascent capitalism, as he was at the time occupied with the study of another subject—the Russian village.

III   A *Distinguished Critic of the Western World*

Uspensky's travels abroad enriched his knowledge of Western Europe and enabled him to better evaluate European democracy and civilization, the results of past revolutions, world politics, and international events. This problem of the Western world was in his mind not only in the 1870's—as may be seen from his works *Sick Conscience*, "There They Know," and "Diary of a Provincial Abroad." He was preoccupied with the same problem in the following years as well (in *Vypryamila*, "Bitter Reproach"—"Gorky upryok," and others), since in the second half of the 1880's Uspensky again went abroad, for the third time.

Uspensky was keenly interested in all important events concerning international politics and economic conditions of his time. He read books about the industrial revolution, capital-ism, and socialism, and some works by Marx and Engels; he gave much thought to the French Revolution and the Paris Commune; he closely followed new developments in science and technology; he studied factory legislation and parliamentary reports. His own observations of life in Paris, London, and other large Western European cities, his visit to Constantinople, his travels in Denmark, Serbia, and other places were all reflected in his works of the 1870's and 1880's. His descriptions and observations of foreign customs and manners, world politics, international events were invariably keen, fresh, and bold; they were timely and instructive.

For example, in the sketch "Unusual Situation" ("Neprivychnoe polozhenie") (1887), Uspensky defended the right of each nation to freedom and independence. He passionately condemned the colonial policy of tsarist Russia and other countries and was deeply pained as he watched the rise of nationalism and militarism after the fall of the Paris Commune. He was glad when the people of various nationalities—contrary to the policies of their government—came out for friendship, fraternity, and peace among nations. He was angered and revolted by the policy of the "three emperors" whom he called the "trinity" of huge fists formed by the "friendly handclasp of the three monarchs of Germany, Italy, and Austria..." ("The Desert River—Migrants in Tomsk") ("Reka-pustynya—Pereselentsy v Tomske"). Concerned about the fate of mankind, Uspensky called attention to the aggressive plans of Bismarck, saying that within the borders of the German Empire there "already appeared the sparkling tips of bayonets" (*Visits to the Migrants*) (*Poezdki k pereselentsam*). He saw a sign of the times in the fact that German nationalists presented the chancellor with an "iron bouquet" ("So Far") ("Poka-chto' "). In the article "The Fall of Bismarck and the Revival of the San Stefano Treaty" (written in 1890, but not published at that time), Uspensky rejoiced over the removal of Bismarck. In his view, this meant a victory for Russia and for all people of Europe.

Uspensky noted three forces at work in Europe: There was Bismarck's Germany with its aggressive designs creating tension in international relations; commercial and industrial England was busy taking care of its colonial possessions ("It's Quiet with Man") ("S chelovekom-tikho"); and in France,

sinister tendencies were on the rise while the great ideas of
fraternity, equality, and liberty proclaimed in 1789 were being
forgotten. In his "Diary of a Provincial Abroad" (1876) Uspensky, speaking about French politics of the 1870's, pointed out
that in France good men like François-Vincent Raspaille, who
actively participated in the revolutions of 1830, 1848, and 1871,
were now in jail and barred from taking part in the country's
political life. Their places were taken by persons like Léon
Gambetta, who refused to vote for amnesty for the Communards.
Uspensky imagined the day when such Deputies would be
asked by the electorate:

Have you done at least one thing that featured so prominently in
your preelection programs? . . . "No," you will say, "we have not
done anything like this. We were simply smart and conducted our-
selves so cleverly and with such subtlety that the Senate no longer
takes notice of our existence." (VI, p. 63)

Uspensky gave a penetrating analysis of the essence of
"Boulangerism" which ruled French political life in the 1880's.
The strangler of the Paris Commune and advocate of revenge,
General Boulanger, nicknamed "General Revenge," was War
Minister in 1885-1887. In his journalistic notes, Uspensky showed
how French bourgeois society and various French parties were
hoping to find in Boulanger a faithful spokesman for their political ambitions. The result was that the General-Minister became
a tool of these parties—a "figure" called upon to preside over
the economic and political rebirth of France ("Ashinov and
Boulanger," 1889).

Uspensky clearly understood the significance of the ideas of
the great French Revolution for the advance of mankind. He
also understood the importance of the subsequent revolutionary
struggles of the French people. However, the revolutions had
led to only a slight improvement in the lot of the workers,
whose interests were ignored and betrayed. This was the theme
of Uspensky's tale "At An Old Place Burned Out By Fire"
(1876). Revolution, Uspensky wrote—after convincing the poor
working class that they were not animals, but human beings—
had "nevertheless failed to provide them with any security;
it has left them alone in the middle of the road saying: 'Well,
brother, now go and live as best you can'" (IV, p. 119). The

words "Liberty, Equality, Fraternity," said Uspensky in his sketch "Ashinov and Boulanger" were even now "painted on every wall," but it was there that the police dragged free citizens by the collar. Uspensky condemned this hypocritical world which covered lies with beautiful, meaningless words. "Good words, but ugly deeds," he commented (XI, p. 559).

It is significant that in his article "Bitter Reproach" (1888), Uspensky treated the French workers' movement as the outcome of the European capitalist system as a whole. He pointed out that the movement spelled great danger for this system and therefore could not but arouse alarm and evoke ruthless action on the part of Franco-Prussian reactionaries.

Uspensky turned to Karl Marx's writings on this subject. Uspensky's interest in the works of this economist and scholar can be noted as early as the 1870's. In "Bitter Reproach" written in the 1880's Uspensky directly borrowed the opinions of Marx concerning conditions in Russia and Western Europe. He wrote:

In the brochure written together with Engels for the purpose of explaining the bloody Parisian massacre, it was clearly shown how France and Germany cooperated behind the scenes in their joint suppression of this uprising; for this uprising is the product of the European capitalist system, which caused both of these countries to feel alarmed. At the same time as "nations" they were enemies and every now and then their soldiers hit at each other under the walls of Paris, chiefly "for the newspapers" and for the sake of observing diplomatic formalities. (XII, p. 12)

Thus, Uspensky's approach in evaluating the results of social developments in industrially advanced Western European countries was a highly skeptical one. This skepticism is especially noticeable in Uspensky's descriptions of his impressions of the Eiffel tower ("Machine and Man") and the Statue of Liberty ("Supplement to the Story 'Receipt'") ("Dopolneniye k rasskazu 'Kvitantsiya'"). This does not mean, however, that Uspensky saw the Western world, bourgeois democracy, and bourgeois revolutions in a totally negative light. He did not glorify Russia. He understood that Russia—without repeating the mistakes of Western Europe or abandoning its own path of development— must take into account the "great experience of European life," that part of the experience which could, indeed, be of use to the workers. He was convinced that the bourgeois-democratic system of his time did show some concern for the well-being of workers, even if it did lead to public discussions of problems relating to the everyday life and work of the people in Russia who were still known as "unwashed mugs" and "drunkards." What attracted Uspensky abroad was the very fact that there the fight for the interests and rights of working people had already begun. Uspensky was glad to see that Western "workers who took part in protests believed in their cause" though "knowing that it is neither today nor tomorrow that anything will come out of the fight" (XI, p. 556). But it was nevertheless important that there were results, however small, and these results inspired a further drive and struggle for greater results.

The situation was quite different in Russia, where this process was still in its first stage. Russian society was offered, Uspensky observed ironically—as an ideal—love for stock dividends, but under the condition that this love would not lead to awkward consequences. "We will adopt every European evil, but any European measure against that evil is unacceptable, and we will manage things in such a way that everybody will mind his own business and not bother about what doesn't concern him" (XII, pp. 14-15).

What Uspensky wanted to say here is clear: Abroad, there was struggle against the evil of capitalism. This struggle determined the character of Western European life and made relations between people clear. In Russia, there was no such struggle; on the contrary, the rejection of struggle was preached as an ideal. This circumstance, noted Uspensky, explained the "stagnation of our life" and the "abominable habit of fussing about things." Though the "dragging out of one's life," for the sake of this ideal—that is, it was permissible to manufacture, but not to struggle against the evil it brought about—could possibly be accepted as a way of leading a "quiet and elegant existence," it would be a crime and a great sin to be at peace with such a life and such an ideal. Uspensky called for getting rid of such deceptive and false "elegance."

It can be seen, then, that Uspensky did not glorify Russia while belittling Western Europe, though he did find something at home—the peasant communal way of life—which seemed to provide the answer to the question troubling mankind.

CHAPTER 4

Utopian Ideal and Realistic Method

"... the real truth of life led me to its source,
i.e., to the peasant."

I *Populist Socialism and Uspensky.* From a Village Diary

THE programmatic declaration by Uspensky quoted above
is from his *Autobiography* and immediately follows descriptions of his impressions abroad. The conception of a utopian
"peasant paradise" began to form in Uspensky's mind as a result
of his observations of bourgeois development in Western Europe
and capitalist development in Russia. Uspensky did not find
"real truth," that is, happiness of the working man, in the
Western world. The ruthless suppression of the Paris Commune
and the wave of reaction that swept Europe in the 1870's, the
desperate situation of the workers, and the insignificant gains
they achieved after many revolutions made Uspensky cautious
and skeptical in approaching Western Europe, leading him to
reach some bitter conclusions.

Between 1872 and 1876 Uspensky was, in a sense, in the
same position as Alexander Herzen had been in the 1850's
following the suppression of the 1848 Revolution. Like Herzen,
Uspensky, too, saw hopes for a better future in the way of life
of the Russian village through the strength of the peasant masses.
And indeed, when he set about discovering the "secret of the
people's strength," that is, the strength of the peasant masses,
it was to Herzen that he turned, who first suggested the idea
of utopian socialism based on the peasant way of life in Russia.

In his *Autobiography* Uspensky speaks about his being attracted to the peasant, not only in the intellectual and moral, but
particularly in a personal sense. Uspensky felt in the peasant
masses a certain healing strength that would be able to save
all—almost the whole world. In a letter (1875) to his wife he

61

wrote: "In Russia the only livable place is the village. This civilized society is a horrible bore" (XIII, p. 183).

In the summer of 1877 Uspensky "went to the people." He stayed at the Valdaika railway junction in the village of Sopka in Novgorod Province; from March 1878 to the summer of 1879 he and his family lived near Samara in the village of Skolkovo where he worked as a clerk in a bank. After leaving Samara Province, Uspensky lived at the Lyadno Farmstead near Chudovo railway junction, and in 1881-82 he first rented and then bought a small house in the village of Syabrintsi in the same region. The house became, for many, a second Yasnaya Polyana: they went there to see Uspensky, to pay their respects, to seek his advice on how one should live and what one should do, or simply to have a rest after serving their terms in the Kresty prison.[1]

It was not by accident that Uspensky went to live in Samara Province. Several members of *Zemlya i volya* settled there in those years, among them, Ivanchin-Pisarev, Bogdanovich, Alexander K. Solovyov, S. Leshern, and Vera Figner. A seminary student, A. Aleksandrovsky, who had been tried for his revolutionary activities, worked as Uspensky's helper in the bank in Skolkovo.

In Novgorod Province, Uspensky also had a wide circle of friends from among the revolutionaries. The Lyadno Farmstead where he stayed belonged to A. V. Kamensky, a friend, who was associated with Populist groups and was at the time under police surveillance. Here Uspensky met Lopatin and N. Griboedov, who took part in drawing up the plan for the release of Chernyshevsky. Many revolutionaries came to see Uspensky in Syabrintsi. Ivan I. Popov, a member of *Narodnaya volya*, came here secretly on behalf of Pyotr F. Yakubovich, the poet-revolutionary, and gave Uspensky a copy of an issue of that organization's publication.[2] There is evidence that Vera Figner was also in Syabrintsi at the time. Grigory A. Machtet, the writer and democrat—who wrote the song "I am Tormented by Captivity"—which became highly popular in revolutionary circles, came here immediately after returning from exile in Siberia.

While living in Novgorod and Samara Provinces, Uspensky not only observed village life, but was in close contact with the revolutionaries of the time, and came to share the ideas and feelings of the Populists. Their struggle and sufferings became part of his own life; their fate became his personal concern.

On the basis of his observations of peasant life and his daily contact with peasants, Uspensky—in the late 1870's and early 1880's—worked out a philosophy based on Russian village life and created a new literary genre, that of cyclical sketches on village life. They include *From a Village Diary* (*Iz deprevenskogo dnevnika*)' (1877-78), *Peasant and Peasant Labor* (*Krestyanin i krestyansky trud*) (1880), *The Power of the Soil* (*Vlast zemli*) (1882), *From Conversations with Friends* (*Iz razgovorov s priyatelyami*) (1883), on the theme of the power of the soil, and others.

The principal idea underlying these works is the opposite of that found in *Ruin*. There the worker, Mikhail Ivanovich, went to St. Petersburg to seek his mentor, the *raznochinets*, Maxim Petrovich, who had awakened his self-awareness. The theme reflects the revolutionary-democratic ideology of the 1860's. The theme is reversed, as it were, in Uspensky's cycles of sketches of the village, for this time, the *raznochinets*, Uspensky, in his search for the "real truth" and "a humane way of life" opposed to the "cruel truth" of Western Europe, turned to the Russian village, to "the source"—the peasant, to the "just life of the people." Uspensky tried to discover in the strenuous life of the peasant and in his outlook a pattern for the future and a basis upon which to build his ideal and his philosophy of life. Here one can see the link between Uspensky and the Revolutionary-Populist ideology of the 1870's and 1880's.

The link, however, was an extremely complex one, for Uspensky had at the same time profound doubts about Populist ideas and some of his views were sharply anti-Populist. Uspensky had never been a Populist, strictly speaking; he did not belong to the Populist Movement of the 1870's and 1880's. His writings of those years cannot be considered part of the Populist movement or the outgrowth of Populist ideology. Even in his most Utopian works, such as the article "By the Labor of One's Own Hands" ("Trudami ruk svoikh") (1884), Uspensky was concerned not so much with showing how "to live a holy life" as how the workers of Russia actually lived. One cannot begin to understand Uspensky's works of those years, his spiritual and moral outlook, and his thinking, unless one takes into account

the fact that Uspensky was in a constant state of conflict, restlessness, tension, and development, boldly striking out in search of
new ideas and travelling around Russia. One must bear in mind
that Uspensky lived and worked at a critical moment in the
intellectual life of Russia, the moment when the illusions of
Utopian Peasant Socialism were being shattered and the idea
of Scientific Socialism began to emerge.

In turning to the village, Uspensky was not merely being
influenced by Populist ideology. The years in which his village
sketches appeared (1877-1882) coincided with another revolutionary period (1879-1881) during which the hardships of village
life and the needs of the village became widely known. The
cruel and repulsive "truth" in the bourgeois West, the Russian
village once again making known its needs, the steadfast development of capitalism in Russia, and the whole logic of Uspensky's
spiritual search inevitably pushed him into the arms of the
peasant and awakened in him the desire to understand, on the
basis of his own observations and without prejudice, what the
Russian village was really like, and to find out whether the
Populist, the Slavophile, and official views which were prevalent
at the time, were well-founded. Like the participants in the
movement of "going to the people" and the intellectual members
of *Zemlya i volya*, Uspensky—on "the road to the village"—experienced many bitter disappointments. And this is fully understandable since Uspensky, unlike the Populists, did not write
off the development of capitalism in Russia.

Referring to his opponents in the Populist camp who sharply
criticized and repudiated his sketches *From a Village Diary*
Uspensky wrote:

To our tired society came the thought of stopping the flywheel of
the European system which captivated us as we went about our
way of lies and deceits—though, of course, we hate lies and deceits
and wish to live honorably, according to our conscience.... And
so people started throwing into the cogs of the wheel all kinds of
obstacles which, however, failed to do their job: the wheel continued
to turn hurling out mostly paper obstacles which were supposed to
have stopped it from turning.... The Slavic race, the Slavic idea,
Orthodoxy, the absence of a proletariat, etc.—all this, written down
on huge quantities of paper, was nevertheless unable to stop the
turning of the wheel which seems to say to the ordinary Russian:

"All this is nonsense! You have a proletariat now, and you will have a big proletariat in the future. . . ." (V, pp. 193-94)

In *From a Village Diary* there was, for the first time in Uspensky's works, a rare specimen of the real peasant. He was Ivan Afanasiev, "a man who in his mind and heart is inseparably linked to the earth," and who would play an important role in Uspensky's future works. Uspensky did not develop the character, but rather gave a highly sympathetic description of what he was like. Ivan Afanasiev did not know how "to be cunning, or to be sly, or to deceive—such skills are not demanded by work with the soil" (V, p. 57).

To Ivan Afanasiev, the soil was what sustained him:

it is the source of joy and misfortune, happiness and sorrow, of all his prayers and gratitude to God . . . Work with the soil and the care and happiness involved in it fill up the entire inner life of Ivan Afanasiev, leaving him no opportunity to think about the possibility of doing any other kind of work besides farming . . . Ivan Afanasiev is not in love with the soil. . . . no, he is linked to it, to all that it goes through in the course of a year, linked to it as a husband is linked to his wife, even closer, since Ivan Afanasiev and the soil live almost as one.
And Ivan Afanasiev was not " 'chained' to the soil. . . ." Working with the soil is dear to him, in the sense that the relationships between the man and the soil, between the man and his work are not forced, in the sense that the link between them is clean. . . . On these clean, honorable foundations rests the way of life of the genuine, unspoiled peasant family. . . .

The work of a farmer, said Uspensky in a manner reminiscent of folk verse, linked the farmer's "soul with the sky, the earth, the red sun, clear dawns, blizzards, rain, snow storms, frost, with all that is created by God with all the wonders of this godly creation . . ." (V, p. 54).

But as Uspensky came to know the Russian village well, he saw that the ruble was as powerful here as elsewhere, that the drive for the ruble competed successfully with Ivan Afanasiev's attachment to the earth and to his work with the soil. Under the influence of the new age with its constant cry: "Let's have money!" Ivan Afanasiev found it "necessary to do everything he could in order somewhere, somehow to get this damned silver ruble into his hands. The "erosion" of the roots of the peasant outlook was also dealt with in Uspensky's other works (*Peasant and Peasant Labor,* and *The Power of the Soil*). A terrifying and disturbing question rose before Uspensky: Would the people be able to stand up "under the pressure of the ruble?" (VIII, p. 80).

In *From a Village Diary* Uspensky tore off the pretty veil through which the Populists viewed the village. That is, he shattered the Utopian belief that the peasant was a Natural Socialist. The whole style and tone of the work conveys a documentary truthfulness. Uspensky recorded, day after day, in a concise manner, at times in the form of notes, what he observed about the life of the villages in Novgorod and Samara Provinces. The "diary" consists of two parts: "In the Northern Zone" (Novgorod Province) and "In the Steppes" (Samara Province). Although natural conditions in the two regions were different—they were unfavorable for agriculture in the northern zone, but favorable in the steppes—the economic and social conditions of the peasant in the two provinces were similar. The two parts are made up of "fragments" (three in the first and six in the second part), each of which consists of short sketches, notes, descriptions of scenes, reflections by the author, analysis of facts about the villages, short tales, and most frequently—dialogues. In this form of literary composition the material is treated in a free manner, which Uspensky considered necessary for his purpose.

He showed that the communal basis of village life was a fiction, that it was certainly not the determining factor in the life of the village, and that the pursuit of money had destroyed the world of the village. Uspensky concluded that there were as many, or "almost as many" "Western European ulcers" in Russia as in "their place of origin" (V, p. 195). Historically, this was a correct and profound materialistic explanation of the psychological and moral dependence of the Russian peasant on what was taking place in the village. Here, however, Uspensky fell into a serious conflict characteristic of his thinking. He tried to resist those aspects born of the socio-economic conditions of the village undergoing capitalistic changes, with the belief that in human relations there must be truthfulness, humaneness, and integrity. With this conviction Uspensky called on the intelligentsia to bring light to the village, to teach the peasants to lead a life based on reason and conscientiousness. But even as he tried to rouse the intelligentsia, he realized the utopian character and the futility of his calls.

II   Peasant and Peasant Labor

Summing up his observations and thoughts at the time he was writing *From a Village Diary*, Uspensky noted in his *Autobiography*: "Unhappily, I was in such places where the source was not evident.... But it was necessary for me to know the source of ... the cunning mechanism of the life of the people, for which I could not find any simple explanation anywhere" (IV, p. 579).

In 1880 Uspensky published his second cycle of sketches about the village: *Peasant and Peasant Labor*. In this work the economic and social conditions of the life of the peasant were interpreted differently from those in *From a Village Diary*. While writing the *Diary*, Uspensky lived in Novgorod Province near the railway; he stayed at places where money had already become the new god and ruled the soul and action of the peasant. The second time Uspensky was in Novgorod Province, he lived in an out-of-the-way place, at the Lyadno Farmstead near the Chudovo Railway Junction where only one peasant family lived. Uspensky wrote in his *Autobiography*:

In my eyes the wild, remote place became alive under the plow of the tiller, and it was then that I, for the first time in my life, really saw a truly important feature of the life of the Russian people— that is, the power of the soil. (XIV, pp. 579-80)

In his memoirs, Uspensky's brother, I. I. Uspensky, told that the Lyadno Farmstead was looked after by a peasant named Leonty Osipovich Belyaev, who served as the prototype of Ivan Ermolaevich, the main character in *Peasant and Peasant Labor*. This opinion was shared by L. K. Chermak, a student at the Petrovskaya Agricultural Academy, who knew Uspensky well in Novgorod Province.[3]

It could be said that this time Uspensky observed village life under special conditions. These conditions, however, were typical of the entire patriarchal Russia which was on its way out. In *Peasant and Peasant Labor* Uspensky saw hope for

the future in the conscious and free development of ideals
formed in the pre-capitalist, patriarchal conditions of the
Russian village. It is common knowledge that after the 1861
reform, as capitalism began to develop in Russia, the village
was not a united community. The peasantry was split into
poor peasants or village proletarians, and kulaks or well-to-do
peasants. Uspensky showed this process of the disintegration
of peasantry with great truthfulness and at the same time
with a profound sense of uneasiness in *From a Village Diary*,
his first important work about the Russian village. He was
frightened and deeply disturbed by this process, as well as by
the entire process of capitalist development in Russia. Faced
with the disintegration of the village and the triumphant advance
of "Mr. Dividend," Uspensky tried to pin his hopes on the
peasant whose life was yet unaffected by the new social trends,
who was seemingly independent and lived according to the
principle of doing everything by himself, who was yet neither
a proletarian nor a kulak, but threatening to become transformed
—and eventually did become transformed—into one or the other.

Uspensky fell in love with this socially unstable peasant and
gave a vivid portrait of him, first through the character of Ivan
Afanasiev in the *Diary* and later, through Ivan Ermolaevich in
Peasant and Peasant Labor. In these portrayals Uspensky emphasized what he considered to be the ideal that could save mankind—the ideal of a proper life, a life of integrity, based on
working the land with one's own hands. In *Peasant and Peasant
Labor* Uspensky regarded the peasant primarily as a worker of
the soil, whose occupation was with nature. Uspensky's aim
here was to present the character of Ivan Ermolaevich as a
typical farmer.

The author of *Peasant and Peasant Labor* was not merely an
observer of village life who kept a diary, but someone who
entered into direct, close contact with peasants. He tried to
understand not just a few isolated facts about them, but the
inner meaning of their village life and the influences affecting
that life. The work unfolds gradually like a novel with detailed
descriptions, both analytical and lyrical.

Uspensky showed that Ivan Ermolaevich struggles not merely
for the sake of getting a piece of bread and paying taxes—as
he had believed earlier—but that all the peasant's feelings,

thoughts, and concerns were tied up with his work which gave him a sense of moral and even esthetic satisfaction. Ivan Ermolaevich, according to Uspensky, lived a full and sensible life. Within the sphere of agricultural labor his thinking was free, bold, and clear. The essence of all this was what Uspensky called "the poetry of working with the soil." In a letter, Uspensky suggested that the reading of the third chapter of *Peasant and Peasant Labor* be accompanied by a careful reading of the poem "Harvest," ("Urozhay") by the outstanding Russian poet Alexey V. Koltsov (1809-42). Uspensky wrote: "That's where one finds something fully harmonious and complete, without any talk about 'communities' or the mysterious spirit of the people and so on" (XIII, p. 378).

Uspensky's interpretation of peasant labor was rejected by his friend, Saltykov-Shchedrin, editor of *Otechestvennye zapiski,* a journal to which Uspensky was a contributor. Saltykov-Shchedrin was opposed to the idea of a peasant Utopia all his life. Not that he failed to see the poetry of working with the soil, but he was above all concerned with the drudgery of peasant life and peasant labor. Uspensky knew, of course, that this poetry was only one aspect of peasant life, but drew his inspiration from his discovery of this poetry in the life of the peasant. And in it Uspensky tried to find the basis for the solution of all questions of peasant life. In 1885, when Uspensky had written other works in which he declared peasant labor to be the means of curing all social and moral ills, Saltykov-Shchedrin published a fable, *Konyaga,* in which he poked fun at such futile Utopian dreams.

However, *Peasant and Peasant Labor* is not a narrow work dealing only with the subject of peasant Utopia. What happened was that the Utopia—the wish to find in peasant labor the answer to the question of how to achieve a happy and meaningful life—forced Uspensky to study village life closely, so that he could really understand it and could say truthfully whether the Russian village contained the "pattern" of a humane life, or whether the hopes placed in it were mere fantasies, comfortable self-deception, and "sweet daydreams." Uspensky's Utopia was, therefore, of a peculiar kind, in the sense that Uspensky, while fashioning it, had in mind a living example— the Russian peasant. It was a Utopia that was based on realism;

in fact, it infused into Uspensky's realism a special analytical strength and social alertness. It was a Utopia that demanded true conviction, and the only way of arriving at such a conviction was through an honest analysis of what the village was really like.

As Uspensky saw it, the life of the peasant was conditioned by the work he did. Agricultural labor influenced every aspect of his social and family life. Gorky, who called Uspensky the "distinguished expert" on peasantry and peasant life, noted that Uspensky had a profound understanding of the power of the soil over the peasant and had described that power with great skill.[4] And in so doing Uspensky enriched Russian classical literature. One can also see that Uspensky's approach to the peasant and peasant labor was the opposite of that of the Populists.

In what way, in Uspensky's view, did nature and the soil influence the spiritual world of the peasant? What rules of life did they teach the peasant? The answers, contained in the village sketches, which clearly reflect Populist illusions, are at the same time anti-Populist. The naïvely feudalistic outlook of Ivan Ermolaevich, which grew out of the conditions of nature of farm labor and demanded absolute power for the head of the family, would and did alienate him completely from the revolutionary terrorists. Uspensky saw that the latter did not and could not in their struggle find support among the peasant masses. The ideals of Ivan Ermolaevich ran counter to Populist Utopian Socialism, which was as alien to the peasant as the struggle of the members of *Narodnaya volya*. Living according to old rural ideals, Uspensky pointed out, the peasant "thinks that one's entire life, all one's interests, and delights are to be found in the bustle of one's own backyard" (VII, p. 69).

The peasant-poet portrayed by Uspensky turned out to be a peasant-proprietor who was interested in his personal possessions only and who lived in the village in which capitalism had begun to develop. While Uspensky idealized peasant labor, the basis of Ivan Ermolaevich's life, he was not blind to the prosaic side of his hero. Ivan Ermolaevich had an "aristocratic-peasant soul," but he also had unattractive features. In him there was an odd mixture of patriarchal habits and bourgeois notions about how he should manage his personal property.

His possessive nature was clearly revealed in his relations to the village and particularly to the village poor. The peasant-poet was actually a prudent peasant-proprietor, who saw something in the poor that was alien and hostile to him. It is significant that Uspensky contrasted the interests of Ivan Ermolaevich to those of the poor and ended up on the side of the poor. Uspensky thus showed the splitting of the village into different, and not entirely friendly, groups.

It is clear that Uspensky was torn in his attitude toward his hero. In fact, the hero—the peasant who lived according to the principle of "doing everything by himself"—had ceased to exist as capitalism penetrated the village. Thus, Uspensky's hopes for a life based on working the soil with "one's own hands" could not be realized, since they were unfounded. This was one of the major causes of Uspensky's spiritual torment and eventual breakdown.

But Uspensky did not give up his hopes. He continued to call on the intellectual *raznochintsi* "to go to the people." Why? Uspensky seemed to think—and here he reflected the typical Populist point of view—that it was the intelligentsia's mission to protect and save the ideals of agricultural labor from the pernicious touch of capitalist civilization. However, Uspensky adopted an ironic tone as he condemned this civilization especially in chapters entitled: ("Extenuating Circumstances") ("Smyagchayushchie vinu obstoyatelstva") and ("Bonds of Falsehood") ("Uzy nepravdy"). This is understandable, since Uspensky knew not only the evils of capitalism, but also its benefits—the benefits it brought to that very same Ivan Ermolaevich.

The disintegration of the village with the formation of bitterly hostile camps, the emergence of individualism, and the instincts of private ownership in peasant life disgusted Uspensky. He had wanted to find in the peasant that strength which is the basis of socialism. He even tried to be a propagandist and persuade the peasants to practice collectivism. But the arguments in favor of private ownership in the village at that time were such that Uspensky, like many who "went to the people" and like members of the *Zemlya i volya*, found himself in a blind alley.

"Tell me," said Uspensky to Ivan Ermolaevich, the 'aristocrat of the fields,' "is it not possible to do collectively the work which is beyond the strength of one man?"

"You mean for people to work together?"

"Yes."

Ivan Ermolaevich thought for a while and said,

"No! Where'd that get you? How're you going to do it? Say, you've got ten men and they can't lift one log, but I can carry it like a feather all by myself if I have to. No, how're you going to do it? Then someone will say, 'Let's quit, fellows, and go and have our lunch,' but I want to work. And so what happens? He goes to his lunch, and I'd be working for him. No, it's not possible. How're you going to do it? We're all made different. It'd be like writing one letter for the whole village. . . ." (VII, p. 69)

Thus, Uspensky was painfully mistaken about his idol, who was also the idol of a whole generation of the best people in Russia.

It is clear that Uspensky's idealization of Ivan Ermolaevich did not lead to embellishment or distortion of reality. Uspensky loved the peasant, but he looked at him objectively and saw him as he really was. Uspensky did not close his eyes to the unattractive life and tragic fate of the peasant, and did not seek comfort in the "poetry of working with the soil." He did not evade the political questions involved, and he did not avoid struggle. With sad irony he mocked the Tolstoyans and the Populists who got carried away by the search for the "higher truth," for the formula that would show them "how to live a holy life," forgetting how the working people actually lived (IX, pp. 271, 280).

Having shown that the peasants of his time were not thinking about socialism based on agricultural labor as taught by the Populists, Uspensky sought to find out what the peasants actually lived by and what they wanted. Uspensky saw that it was the "passionate expectation of land" that united the peasant masses. "In the course of twenty years," he pointed out, "the peasants have pursued one real, definite aim expressed by the demand for increasing the allotment of land. For twenty years, without a pause, they have reiterated one thing: 'We have too little land!'"(VII, pp. 90-91). This problem of land, not only as one with philosophical, moral, and psychological

implications, but also as an economic and social question, became one of the major subjects of Uspensky's works. In his
writings about the village, Uspensky began to demand, persistently, fervently, and angrily, land for the peasant masses, citing
reasons that touched all fields: political and economic, national
and state, ethical, sociological, philosophical, and esthetic.

In showing the fallacy of Utopian Peasant Socialism, in help-
ing to make the democratic intellectuals of his time see the
error of the Populist program for saving Russia, and in pointing
out the real needs of the village, Uspensky contributed to the
advance of the revolutionary liberation movement and the development of socialist thought in the 1870's and 1880's. All
this, however, is about the objective meaning of his village
sketches.

Subjectively, Uspensky was unable to give up his hopes about
the countryside, unable to pursue his thoughts to their logical
end and, without fear and without any feelings of regret,
unable to face the conclusions to which he himself had led his
readers. Though he clearly saw that the socialist hopes of the
revolutionaries of his time were groundless, he nevertheless
could not bring himself to condemn them or himself. To do so
would be to lose those hopes which alone had kept him alive,
forcing him to grapple with problems, to think, to suffer, and
to write. Uspensky had always known, however, that his hopes
would not be realized, that they were fated to remain only
aspirations. Capitalist Russia was steadily destroying the patriarchal village, thus destroying the basis of what lay most
closely to his heart.

III The Power of the Soil

In the two cycles of village sketches discussed above, the
power which held Ivan Ermolaevich to this world is not yet
concretely described. In Uspensky's third cycle of village
sketches, *The Power of the Soil* (*Vlast' zemli*), published in
1882, this mysterious and tremendous power is fully revealed
through the dramatic story of the life of the peasant Ivan Bosykh.
Uspensky, like Nekrasov, in portraying the might of the peasantry, recreated the folk epic about Svyatogor the Defender.[5]
This epic contains "the whole essence of the life of the people."

Anyone reading this folk epic carefully, said Uspensky, would
see that

everything in it is deeply thought out; everything in it had great
significance for the understanding of the essence of the life of the
people: the weight and the power of the soil are enormous, so
enormous that red blood rushed to the hero's face when he attempted
to move [the purse] even a little, and yet the people carry this
burden and power as lightly as they would an empty purse. (VIII,
p. 27) [Note: The "purse" in question was filled with earth. Ed.]

Uspensky was the first in the history of Russian literature to
portray the power of the soil over the peasant, even though
there had been others before him who had drawn attention to
the influence of agricultural labor on peasant psychology, among
them Dmitry V. Grigorovich, author of *The Tiller* and *The Tiller
and the Master*.

The organization of *The Power of the Soil*, which Vladimir
Korolenko called "a philosophy and an epic poem of agricultural
labor," was determined by Uspensky's aim, that of describing
clearly and convincingly the importance of the soil. The first six
chapters of the work deal with the power of the soil in its
"cleansed form"; the last chapters (beginning with the chapter
"Now and Then") deal with that "harsh reality" which under-
mined the "power of the soil," scattered the "golden grains,"
and threw away the "pearl" that lay hidden in the heart of the
peasants' way of life.

As he went deeper into the question of the secret of the
people's strength, Uspensky was not free from exaggeration,
simplification, and errors. He tended to overemphasize the influence of agricultural labor and the power of the soil over man
and society as a whole. Occasionally, instead of examining the
question from a concrete, historical point of view, he idealized
the man who was under this power. In *The Power of the Soil*
Uspensky went even further in his idealization of the peasant
and agricultural labor, declaring that "agricultural labor alone
is sinless—holy labor, placing the farmer's private and social
relations in sinless, innocent forms" (VIII, p. 73). Uspensky
was convinced that agricultural labor gave "full scope" to one's
intelligence, strength, creative abilities, and talent. He described
the agricultural labor of his time as "many-sided" labor and

spoke of the "harmony of agricultural labor." Peasant labor demanded the *"whole* man" who "did everything himself"; the man who did agricultural labor was a "whole human being," and not just a shoemaker, a bootmaker, or a telegraph operator.

The Power of the Soil, however, is not only about the peasant who, according to Uspensky, represented the highest type of man. It also shows the actual social and economic conditions under which agricultural labor was performed. The power of the soil was not the sole force in the village; there was the power of money and the new order that was destroying the power of the soil, and tearing peasants away from agricultural labor. Uspensky struggled to preserve the "pearl" in peasant life—work with the soil; he tried to outline a practical program for saving this "pearl." And all the time he realized the impossibility of attaining his goal in the social and economic conditions which existed in the village after 1861.[6]

Uspensky showed great perception in dealing with the "agricultural type" and the "agricultural outlook." When he came to this question he not merely idealized, but became sharply critical. Speaking of those features in the life of the people that were formed by the power of the soil, Uspensky cited Tolstoy's character in *War and Peace,* the peasant Platon Karataev, whose "spiritual characteristics," said Uspensky, "were derived from the very heart of nature, from centuries-old, constant contact with it, with its eternal kindness and enmity."

Loving nobody in particular, neither himself nor others, Karataev is useful and can do whatever he is told to do: "Take them and tie them ... Take them and untie them ..." "Shoot it," "Free it," "Beat it," or "Save it," "Jump into the water, jump into the fire and rescue someone!" All this he does because nothing means very much to him—neither I, nor that which life gives. ... (VIII, p. 119)

This critical comment shows that Uspensky realized the limitations of the type of people formed by "mother nature."

Though Uspensky was impressed with Karataev, he did not idealize him. Instead, he pointed out the need to change the type of men formed under conditions of agricultural labor. Uspensky wisely observed that the meek and submissive Karataev fattened the world of exploiters and oppressors, and he believed that one must stand up for all the Karataevs and reeducate

them. He considered it to be the duty of the intelligentsia to
carry out the noble tasks of bringing science and culture to the
peasants, of satisfying their urgent need for land, and easing
their labor. But reality continued to frustrate Uspensky's program of calling on the intellectuals to transform the "brutal
truth" about village life into a humane truth.

IV Uspensky's Dream of a Life Based on "Labor of One's Own Hands" with the Soil

In both Russian life and literature of the past there existed
a type of good man, a peculiar kind of Utopian philosopher who
came from the peasantry and who often clothed his dreams of a
paradise-on-earth in religious terms. Such dreams reflected the
fear and confusion of the masses in the face of capitalism, their
protest against the evils in life, their rejection of an unjust
system, their search for deliverance, and finally, their ignorance
of the true ways of attaining salvation. The futile and naïvely
Utopian striving of peasant democrats of the nineteenth century
toward a life "that is godly, based on reason and honor"—according to Nekrasov—also had a certain influence on Uspensky.
Uspensky eagerly studied everything that reflected the search
by the people for a happy life without sin, which gave him
rich material for thought on the ideal forms of communal life
and for constructing his plan of bringing salvation to the working
class.

Uspensky constantly kept in mind the feelings and moods of
the masses searching for an earthly paradise. He contrasted the
capitalist system "which destroys the human personality" to
a system of life based on labor, a life of freedom for all, in which
man, by working on the land which belonged to him, could "feel
himself a whole number and not a fraction, could live without
purchasing someone else's labor or selling his own, that is,
live and preserve his conscience and fully satisfy its needs"
(Supplement to the tale "Receipt," X_2,* p. 130). These thoughts
were linked to Uspensky's deep and lasting interest in the life
of the people in outlying districts of Russia where the power of

---

*The number "1" or "2" indicates "Book One" or "Book Two" in
the volume.

the landowner, the kulak, and the bureaucrat had not penetrated, and where no authority of any kind existed. Uspensky lovingly described the independent and healthy life of the peasants living in the former black earth zone in Russia, who founded a free community in the Altai Mountains (*A Letter from a Journey*) —(*Pisma s dorogi*). Because of his interest in the search for an "earthly paradise" by the people and his desire to work out ideal forms of communal life, Uspensky also studied the life of the religious sects, the *raskolniki* (Old Believers). This sect had its own customs and traditions, free from the authority of parasitic and greedy administrators, from meddling by society, and the influence of advanced civilization. Uspensky's descriptions of the life of the sects showed that the people constituted a great creative force, and that they had the desire and ability to cope with the tasks of creating and upholding a social and economic system under which people would not lose their humaneness.

Uspensky did not idealize the sects. He did not approve of everything they did, but he respected and valued the fact that members of the sects strived toward an intelligent life and asked questions about the "meaning of their existence on earth." This was just what was lacking in the villages in the main provinces of Russia which had been debased by the kulaks, the tsarist administrators, the innkeepers, and the rules imposed on communities by serfdom. In his short article, "Village Schismatics" ("Derevenskie raskolniki") (1891), Uspensky refuted the official and "biased ideas" about the religious *Raskol* (the old faith), pointing out that the most important factors about life in the villages of the *raskolniki* on the Volga were not religious and mystical delusions—these were not what held together the free village communities on the Volga—but independence and new and better conditions of economic, social, and family life. The peasants yearned for an independent economic life; they sought to replace overtaxed communities with free associations. The sects strived for "common prosperity and well-being," and for a "disciplined life" that would ensure "intelligent relations between people."

Uspensky approached the *Raskol* and the religious sects from a standpoint which permitted him to see and understand the real strivings of the peasantry, efforts which were clothed in religious forms. What attracted Uspensky about a sect called "*Obshchie*" ("Common"), which he described in his sketch "Several Hours with Members of a Sect" (1888), was not the rites it practiced, but the economic basis of its life—which was different from that in the rest of the country—and the purity of socio-moral relations between its members. Uspensky was gratified by the "communistic" principles of this community, by its concern about man, about its material well-being and independence, and its striving "to establish honest relations between people." It pained him that this sect-community, under the pressure of government persecution and the influence of new tendencies, had fallen into decay. Nevertheless, the old customs that had been preserved there filled him with enthusiasm; they made him hope that the kind of human relations existing in this community would exist throughout the country.

In his search for ideal forms of communal life based on the "healthy truth of relations" between people, Uspensky turned to the writings of peasants.[7] Once Uspensky came upon a piece of "contemporary people's writing": "The Triumph of the Farmer, or Diligence and Parasitism" by T. M. Bondarev.[8] In it, said Uspensky, " 'glimmers' a certain light, permitting us to glimpse the outline of something bright—a harmonious, just, and extraordinary brightness" (IX, p. 90).

Bondarev's piece made a great impression on Uspensky and once more caused him to feel that the people had a deep yearning for a just way of life. In 1884, Uspensky wrote a pamphlet, "By the Labor of One's Own Hands" in which he gave a theoretical basis for a Utopia founded on peasant labor. After reading the pamphlet, Leo Tolstoy also became interested in Bondarev's ideas and in Bondarev as a person, and wrote an article "Diligence or the Triumph of the Farmer," which was published as a sequel to Bondarev's work and appeared in an abridged form in the newspaper, *Russkoe delo* (1886, No. 12).

To understand Uspensky's feelings about a peasant Utopia, it is necessary to consider his social, moral, and esthetic views. These views, formed in the 1870's as a result of his deep disappointment with the Western way of life which had lost all poetry, holiness, and harmony, led Uspensky to search, tirelessly and eagerly—and at that time, hopelessly—for ways of achieving harmony in life, in social relations, and in human personality. In his article "G. I. Uspensky as Writer and Man" Nikolay G. Mikhaylovsky correctly noted: "The general principle to which all the anxieties of Uspensky can be reduced is the principle of harmony, of balance."[9]

The idea of harmony expressed in the imaginative and journalistic works of Uspensky received little attention in contemporary literary histories, though there is no question that the idea lies at the heart of Uspensky's social, moral, and esthetic ideals, and of his dream of a life based on "labor by one's own hands" with the soil, a life worthy of man in the full sense of that word. Uspensky sought, on the one hand, "the fullest development of the individual" and on the other hand, "social conditions that would allow the fullest development of the individual" (IX, p. 268).

In trying to solve this basic problem of socialism, Uspensky turned to peasant life and practice, to the revolutionary struggle of the intelligentsia, and theoretical studies and imaginative literature dealing with the subject. He treasured everything that seemed to him to uphold his dream of a life in which there would be no exploitation of man by man, in which there would be unity, completeness and harmony in the intellectual, moral, and esthetic spheres. The existing social order—whether it was the capitalist system in the West or the semiserfdom, semibourgeois way of life in Russia—disturbed, oppressed, and tormented him. He rejected the cripple of his day, the man who had been "diminished"; he wanted to rehabilitate him and let him develop fully. He dreamed that there would be harmony between man's duty, will and action for this would enable man to be at peace with himself; this alone would do away with spiritual sickness and abnormality—the absence of inner balance, duplicity, cant, hypocrisy, and falsehood.

Uspensky was repulsed by all kinds of social and moral ugliness of his time—a time when it was possible to combine "humaneness of thought and parasitism of action," when the workers and peasants were left to the mercy of fate, and the intelligentsia dragged out their days unable to find a way to reach the people. In agony and despair, Uspensky searched for means of eliminating the socio-moral antagonisms which were destroying the harmony, balance, and fullness of life—everything that would have made a beautiful life.

To support his idea of a "whole" life based on working the soil with "one's own hands," Uspensky used the "formula for progress" contained in N. Mikhaylovsky's article "What is Progress?" (1869). Uspensky quotes the following from the article:

Progress is the gradual approach toward the wholeness of the indivisible (i.e., the people), toward the fullest possible and all-round division of labor between the organs of man and less and less division of labor between men. All which hampers this movement is immoral, unjust, harmful, and unreasonable. Only that which decreases the multiformity of society thereby enhancing the multiformity of each individual within that society is moral, just, reasonable, and useful. (IX, p. 94)[10]

In his article "By the Labor of One's Own Hands" Uspensky also cited Tolstoy's opinions expressed in "Progress and the Definition of Education" (1862). Somewhat paraphrasing Tolstoy, Uspensky wrote:

Could it be that we Russians are so ignorant and want to remain so ignorant about the situation of our people that we repeat such a senseless and false opinion [Makoley's opinion that the well-being of the workers could be seen through their high wages]? All the people, every Russian without exception, will definitely call that peasant of the steppes rich who has old sheaves of wheat on the threshing floor and who has never known wages, and will definitely call the peasant near Moscow poor who owns a cotton shirt and always receives high wages. In Russia it is not only impossible to determine one's wealth by the wages one receives—one can confidently say that in Russia the appearance of wages is the beginning of diminishing wealth and well-being.

And again: "If someone from among the people wants to read Pushkin's *Boris Godunov* or Solovyov's *History of Russia*, that someone will have to cease being what he is—a man who is independent and able to satisfy all his human wants" (IX, p. 96).[11]

These opinions of Mikhaylovsky and Tolstoy propped up the idea of patriarchal peasant socialism and nourished Uspensky's Utopian dreams. In his article, "By the Labor of One's Own Hands," Uspensky pointed out that Mikhaylovsky's "formula for progress" led "thought which is bewildered to the real path, to the real light" and that Tolstoy's description of the forms of life of the Russian peasantry once and for all "disperses the darkness and fog...which surround literary disputes when the talk is about people and civilization, about Russia and Europe" (IX, p. 95).

Uspensky attached great importance to the fact that the people *"consciously think of truth,* happiness, and independence precisely in terms of a way of life based on the *satisfaction of all one's needs by oneself"* (IX, p. 103).

To help explain his thought Uspensky used the works by three novelists published in *Russkaya mysl* (*Russian Thought*) in 1883-84—*One Joke Too Much* (*Doshutilas'*), *Master and Frosya* (*Magistr i Frosya*), *My Widows* (*Moi vdovy*). Uspensky's conclusion was that the life of a family in cultured society was empty and meaningless. The relation between husband and wife lacked harmony—unlike that between the peasant and his "old woman." In cultured society the woman was too much of a woman, and the man too much of man. The man was further "narrowed by his profession," and thus, men and women lived "extremely one-sided" lives. The way leading out of such an ugly life into the sphere of "harmony" was, said Uspensky, pointed out by the author of the "remarkable literary work, *My Widows.*"[12] When the heroine of the story became a widow she had a choice of leading the empty and dependent life of a woman of fashionable society, to which she belonged, or the life of a peasant which was a life of healthy labor and independence. She chose the latter and lived the life of village widows who were able, without outside help, both to take care of their homes and work, "doing the work of both man and woman" (IX, p. 146).

The article "By the Labor of One's Own Hands" received great attention in literary and various social circles. One who praised it in 1889-90 was Bondarev. Some mocked Uspensky's beliefs; others were puzzled and criticized Uspensky for his Utopian thinking. A student, wrote that the article represented "a step backward towards the old darkness, ignorance, threatening the halt of civilization" (XIV, p. 308).[13]

In his letter to Mikhaylovsky and Skabushchevsky, Saltykov-Shchedrin derided Uspensky's attempt to assume the role of a preacher of an ideal "sinless life" based on the life of the peasant and the ideological works of religious sects. Uspensky's preaching, however, attracted the attention of young Maxim Gorky, who was then searching for ways of carrying out the Socialist ideal. Gorky was fascinated by the idea of farm life based on the "labor of one's own hands" and by Uspensky's call to the intellectuals to defend and uphold his idea. Gorky read with interest Uspensky's sketch "Life of Labor and Life of Toil" ("Trudovaya' zhizn' i zhizn' 'truzhenicheskaya'") (1887), in which Uspensky used part of the material from Timoshchenkov's book *Struggle with Land Predators* (1886), also, a call to a life based on farm labor. The main characters of Uspensky's sketch are Zakhar Zemlya, a peasant, and his comrade Pyotr Volga, a teacher. They led a life which exemplifies Uspensky's ideal of full and all-round spiritual and physical development. Their way of life illustrates Uspensky's Utopian program: they were, in short, ideal peasants who, instead of submitting to the iron laws of capitalism, were able to continue to practice a life based on independent agricultural labor. The sketch impressed young Gorky, who at the time dreamed of setting up an agricultural colony with his friends.[14]

One must not, however, think that Uspensky initiated the idea that intellectuals should settle down in the country and perform agricultural labor. The idea was, in fact, made popular by the Tolstoyans and advocates of various kinds of Utopian socialism. What is more, Uspensky was critical of the ventures of intellectual "volunteers in agricultural work." He regarded such ventures as a useless, even harmful, form of escape under the "healing cover" of the wooden plow, which in the end also provided an excuse for not taking part in politics or public affairs. Commenting on his sketch, "Peasant Women" ("Krestyanskie zhenshchiny") (1890), Vera Zasulich, the revolutionary, noted that Uspensky ridiculed the intellectuals-turned-peasants and saw in their action a desire to build for themselves a "corner" of "buddhistlike tranquility." Uspensky disapproved of the agricultural colonies set up by the Tolstoyans whom he criticized for paying attention to the reactionary side of Tolstoy's teaching only.

After reading Tolstoy's article "What Shall We Do?" ("Tak chtozhe nam delat?")[15] Uspensky wrote in a letter to Ivanchin-Pisarev (April 10-15, 1885) that the Siberian peasant Bondarev had apparently led Tolstoy "out of that nonsense" about charity which he practiced. Now he has only scorn for all that. His call had become: "To the plow!" But I suppose that this won't suit the Count either. So why should he take the routine of the peasant and turn it into something which for him is nothing more than an excuse for not getting involved in politics? For he's not really going to put his hand to the plow. (XIII, p. 448)

The same thought is found in Uspensky's sketch "Dreams" ("Sny") (1884), in which a real tiller said to the intellectual gentleman: "To the plow! . . . You haven't got the right kind of strength for the job. And in this case, sir, the plow can knock you out with one blow. . . . No! sir, this isn't you kind of work" (IX, p. 120).

And yet despite all this, there is a good deal in common between the Utopian ideas found in *The Power of the Soil* and Tolstoy's conviction that the salvation of man lay in agricultural labor. Saltykov-Shchedrin spoke of this similarity in a letter to Mikhaylovsky: "Both Tolstoy and Uspensky rave about the peasant; so we are to think that the peasant is the one who has found the real truth!"[16] But while it is true that Uspensky based his Utopia on peasant labor, he had in mind not peasant labor as performed in his time but labor done under conditions provided by a large, cooperative farm. Thus, Uspensky's idea of a peasant economy was not the same thing as a formal communal organization. Uspensky had always criticized such organizations. In *The Power of the Soil* he asked whether it was justified to describe the existing agricultural routines by such high-sounding and noble words as "commune." Uspensky knew only too well that the peasant community—*obshchina*—of his time was not so much a community as a setup from which taxes were collected. In "Village Diary" Uspensky spoke of peasants being "artificially" united "into associations through the 'mutual guarantee' system in order that they perform all kinds of social duties which for the most part are imposed from without" (V, p. 32). As an alternative to such a taxed community, Uspensky offered the ideal of a free laboring community.

In the chapter entitled "Results and Conclusions," ("Resultaty i zaklyucheniya") in *Peasant and Peasant Labor,* Uspensky said that the *large* communal farm was "something [just] and worthy of praise . . ." (VII, p. 489). Such a farm was where one should lead Ivan Ermolaevich if one wished to "restore" and not "de-

stroy" him. In "Village Diary" Uspensky also noted that "a communal cooperative farm is not only a guarantee from poverty,
but is the only form of social organization capable of providing
general well-being" (V, p. 129).

Tolstoy did not have such ideas. Indeed, such ideas were
betrayed by the "friends of the people"—the liberal Populists.
In the 1880's some of them, including Sergey N. Yuzhakov,
created an idyll of the individual peasant economy, showing
the economic advantages of "working for oneself."[17] From the
standpoint of economic and social conditions in Russia at the
time, Uspensky's hopes for a life based on collective farm labor
may be regarded as unfounded. But looking back today we
may say that Uspensky's "radiant" dream that peasant labor
would become free through socialized means of production
was prophetic. Uspensky's dreams were not false Utopias: They
actually indicate that Uspensky was ahead of his time by anticipating the real demands of the peasant masses.

In his introduction to Nikolay Berdyaev's *Subjectivism and
Individualism in Social Philosophy* (*Subyektivizm i individual-
izm v obshchestvennoy filosofii* (1901), Gleb Struve called Uspensky "an eudaemonist with low demands." In Uspensky, said
Struve, man's striving for happiness appeared in the form of
primitive contentment, of "empirical harmony" which was to
be found in the existing peasant way of life based on the "labor
of one's own hands," a way of life governed by nature. Such
an interpretation of Uspensky's conception of a happy life, however, is wrong. One cannot simply call Uspensky a poet of
beauty, of a ready-made harmony based on agricultural labor,
of the power of the soil. In building his "paradise" Uspensky
did not merely turn to the peasants and nature or adopt an
empirical approach to life, but took into account the intelligentsia, science, progress in production technology, and the
conscious struggle of the working class. He did not look back,
nor did he call for a "paradise" based on patriarchal relations or
submission to nature; he looked ahead and offered a much
needed critique of the ideal life based on the "labor of one's
own hands" and on the "formula for progress" of Mikhaylovsky
and Tolstoy.

The point is that Uspensky did not stop at the ideals expressed
by Ivan Ermolaevich and Bondarev. That is why he became

increasingly skeptical about Mikhaylovsky's "formula for progress" and "natural paradise." Whereas Uspensky took a favorable view of the "formula" in his article "By the Labor of One's
Own Hands" (1884), he almost immediately afterwards came
to doubt its correctness and then rejected it altogether. In the
rough draft for the cycle of sketches entitled *In a Slipshod
Manner (Cherez pen' kolodu)*—a work begun in 1884—Uspensky referred to the "formula" and wrote: "There is nothing new
about this theory of progress. All this is disgusting. . . ." The
words that follow are illegible (IX, p. 636).

Georgy V. Plekhanov, one of the first Russian Marxists, was
correct in saying *"Uspensky showed greatness in his refutation
of Mikhaylovsky."*[18] One should also note the difference between
Uspensky and Tolstoy on the question of the "wholesomeness"
of peasant labor. Uspensky did not deny the antithesis—pointed
out by Tolstoy in his article "Progress and the Definition of
Education"—between the people's way of life and the works
of Pushkin, but to Uspensky this antithesis was not a sign of
"man's moral decline" or the "decline of his spiritual life."
The spiritual needs of the people were so great and their way
of life so imperfect that the people could not become fond of
reading Pushkin without destroying what for Tolstoy were the
ideal forms of life. To Uspensky, Tolstoy's logic concerning people's way of life was unacceptable. Such logic did not trouble
or surprise Tolstoy because to him the common people could
live an independent life and "satisfy all their human needs:
to work, to be merry, to love, to think, and create imaginative
works (like *The Iliad*, Russian songs) . . ."[19]

But Uspensky was preoccupied with the thought of turning
what he considered to be the unstable empirical, unconscious
and unreflecting harmony of peasant life based on "labor of
one's own hands" into a paradise on earth created by man's mind,
will, and struggle. To Uspensky, to bring "light" and "godly
justice" to the village was the highest calling and the most urgent
mission of the Russian progressive intelligentsia.

V *Significance of Uspensky's Village Sketches*

The observations and conclusions contained in *The Power of
the Soil* are of general and fundamental importance for under-

standing both social and economic conditions in the Russian
village after the 1861 reform and life of the peasants in general.

Vera Figner—who met Uspensky in the autumn of 1879—
pointed out in her speech at a meeting held in 1927, marking
the 25th anniversary of Uspensky's death, the sharp differences
between the views of Uspensky expressed in his village sketches
and those of the Populists. For the Socialist Populists, she said,
the village community and artel existing at that time contained
the answers to the future; in their imagination the peasant
appeared bigger than life-size. Uspensky, on the other hand,
spoke about the "brutal morals" of the peasants. "Sincere and
truthful, without any preconceived notions, a sharp and sensitive observer of village life," Uspensky "painted a different picture." He described the "back-breaking physical labor which
barely gave the peasant enough to live on"; he saw the

complete lack of harmony of interests in the village, the inability to
unite forces for the betterment of its life; he portrayed the [peasant's]
slavish submission to nature . . . , the "power of the soil" not only
turned the peasant into a slave of his work, but trained him for a
life of servitude, or submission before every kind of authority.[20]

Uspensky raised the vital questions of his time—though those
were questions which could not be solved then—about life and
work, about the outlook on life and the psychology of millions
of toiling peasants in Russia. For Uspensky it was absolutely
clear that "power is . . . on the side of the millions and not the
hundreds of thousands." He understood that wheat cultivated
by Russian peasants represented an enormous power in international politics, which should be used to promote the well-
being of Russia, and each of her citizens. With a clear realization of the important role of the toiling masses, Uspensky
searched tirelessly for ways—both for himself and for all progressive intellectuals—of reaching the masses. In struggling
against egoistic individualism, Uspensky called attention to
the problem of relations between the intelligentsia and the
people.

In his cycles of village sketches, Uspensky showed the inex-
haustible creative power of the toiling peasant masses, who
deserved a different life than that imposed on them by the
parasitic kulaks, landowners, and the numerous avaricious ad-

ministrative bodies that kept the peasant in a constant state of fear. Uspensky called for an attitude toward the peasant that was sincere, unsentimental, loving, and understanding. He sought to instill in the reader respect for the soil, nature, the peasant, and his work. Work with the soil—but not the back-breaking work of the hired farm laborer—was "saintly" work to Uspensky. Owing to its nature, farm work was different from the degrading fuss over every little penny and every crumb; farm work was noble, fruitful, and highly creative work in which all the possibilities opened up by science and technological inventions could and should be used. In *The Power of the Soil* Uspensky often compared the life and work of the peasant with art—poetry, the performance of an actor, and painting—and through the comparisons showed the poetic and creative nature of the work of the farmer, as well as his independence. To Uspensky the farmer was as creative as the artist, also putting his entire mind and heart in his work.

How to free the peasantry from the brutal "power of the soil" and "power of capital," how to lead it to an understanding of humane truth, and to a life based "not on the penny" but on comradely solidarity, collective labor, and knowledge—these were the questions that confronted and tormented Uspensky. His approach to the question of *"man and nature"* and *"power of the soil"* was unconventional; it arose from conditions in which the Russian peasantry found itself in the second half of the nineteenth century. In the West, the peasant-proprietor had long before this time played his role in the democratic move-ment and had defended his relatively privileged position as compared with that of the proletariat. In Russia, the peasantry was still only on the threshold of a large-scale democratic move-ment. Therefore, it looked forward rather than back. This circum-stance explains the difference between Russian and Western writings on the peasantry, as for example, between Uspensky's *The Power of the Soil* and Zola's *La Terre* (1888).

Zola felt depressed about the life led by French peasants under capitalism. Though he did not exclude the possibility that someday the peasants might "turn everything inside out," for the moment he saw them as conservative, dull, and stupid. Wretched insects crawling about the big and beautiful land—such were Zola's peasants, who, unlike the peasants in Uspensky's work, were not a powerful and united force. According to Zola, the peasantry was ruled entirely by the instinct for personal possessions and had degenerated into mindless, greedy egoists who in the name of "what's mine" and "what's yours" were capable of the cruelest acts in their relation to one another.

To Uspensky, Zola's conception of the "power of the soil" appeared crude and base (XIV, p. 91). But here Uspensky failed to take into account the historical conditions of life of the French peasantry which Zola described in his novel. In Zola, the power of the soil over man was not, as in Uspensky, the power of nature over man which led to the rise of the "agricultural type"; it was chiefly the power of personal property which led to the rise of the peasant-proprietor in whose relation to the soil there was no longer a poetic element. The peasant, as Zola observed, did not notice the beauty of nature. His link with the soil, and his love and affection for the soil were not spontaneous, but coarsened by the feeling of personal property which Uspensky had always regarded as something vile. In Zola, this feeling became an instinct dictating every action of the peasant: his relation with his family, his political and religious outlook, and so on. The tyranny of the "possessive spirit" had killed all the poetry in farm labor, and had destroyed the soil and the man who worked with it. Thus, *La Terre* is not about the poetry of farm labor or the power of nature over the peasant. Instead it tells the tragic story of the division of land in one peasant family.

Of course Uspensky also knew that peasants were capable of cruel acts under the influence of the "possessive spirit." He understood very well how this spirit works and was aware of its economic and social implications. In the village, for example, he had witnessed the rise of hostile groups. However, in the 1870's and even the 1880's, the development of capitalism in the Russian village had not yet completely altered the way of life of the peasant, nor had it turned the majority of peasants into greedy, totally selfish individuals. Uspensky was thus able to find beauty in the "agricultural type"; he was inspired by the peasant who lived by the labor of his hands, in whom he saw a specimen of humane personality. Such a specimen, naturally, did not exist in nineteenth-century France.

The tragedy underlying the question of the soil was also

dealt with by Balzac in his *Les Paysans* (1845). At that time, the majority of French peasants had already fallen under the power of the "demon of personal property." As for Uspensky, he did not ignore the tragic side of the life of the peasant in Russia, but approached the subject from another side. He saw tragedy in the fate of the man who was at the mercy of the power of the soil, of work, and of nature. Uspensky wanted to find a way of freeing the peasant from the fatal power of nature over man.

Uspensky's conception of a happy life—a life based on working the land with one's own hands—invites comparison with the ideas of Thoreau in *Walden* (1854). The two men had one thing in common—their rejection of bourgeois civilization. They were both democratic-minded intellectuals and deeply concerned about the "dehumanization" of man in capitalist society. However, their ideas about how to achieve happiness and be liberated from capitalism are fundamentally different from one another. Both were Utopians, but their Utopias were not the same; and the difference between them reflected the difference between conditions in the Russian village and life on the American farm. Thoreau believed that the reconstruction of life could be carried out through the perfection of the individual which was to be achieved by his own efforts. To Thoreau, the art of living correctly was a personal art. This put him in the camp of Tolstoy rather than of Uspensky. Thoreau built himself a hut in the forest and lived a completely secluded life by the labor of his own hands. This was the kind of "corner" of "Buddhistlike trans-quality" which Uspensky ridiculed. Uspensky also lived in the country, not for the sake of personal salvation and self-perfection, but in order to find a way of freeing the peasant masses from the life they led, of bringing that civilization to them which both Thoreau and Tolstoy rejected. Uspensky, as said earlier, came to preach the idea of collective labor which was again different from the individualistic Utopia of Thoreau.

There are a number of similarities between Uspensky and Thomas Hardy (*Under the Greenwood Tree,* 1872, *Far From the Madding Crowd,* 1874, *The Return of the Native,* 1878, *Tess of the d'Urbervilles,* 1890, and others). What tied the two men was their interest in the conflict between capitalist civilization and the pre-capitalist village. Their approach to the conflict, however, is different. Hardy tended to idealize the person who lived and worked in natural surroundings, unspoiled by city life, bourgeois civilization, and in general the moral standards of a class society which destroyed the charm of the free and unsophisticated life of the "children of nature." Uspensky, on the other hand, was not interested merely in the question of living and working in natural surroundings, free from the bonds of civilization. He was torn by the question of how to give the children of nature the best of civilization, the best that had been thought out and created through the struggle of the common people.

An interesting point emerges from the comparisons between Uspensky and three West European writers (Zola, Balzac, and Hardy). The peasant as portrayed by the Western novelists is always alone, cut off from others, and has no possibility of discussing his problems publicly and openly. For example, another Western writer, Wilhelm von Polentz, in his novel *The Peasant* (1895), showed the tragic loneliness of the German peasant, Butner, in his struggle against the impersonal power of capital. To be sure, the Russian village community after the 1861 reform also offered the peasant little protection from capital and the landowner. The Russian peasants were governed, not by communal principles, but by the laws of the new bourgeois society. Nevertheless, the democratic communal setup which existed then did give a feeling of comradely unity, and inspired hopes for justice, equality, and a belief in the power of the people. All these were, of course, illusions, but they were the kind of illusions that stirred the mind, encouraged struggle, united people, and made them dream about justice and a happy life. The important thing was that unlike the peasant of Zola and Polentz, the Russian peasant did not feel alone. He could always take his grievances to "the people" (*mir*); he was accustomed to discussing problems together with "the people"; and he still did some work collectively with others. All this was of great importance for the future of the peasant in Russia, as well as for literature about him.

The twentieth century saw works whose authors called for the "truth of the dense forest"—for a return to the patriarchal state. These calls prove the irresistible power of the soil over man. An example of such a reactionary Utopian philosophy of life was clearly and skillfully expressed in the novels of Knut Hamsun, *Juices of the Soil,* (1917); *August,* (1930). *Juices of the Soil* has something in common not only with certain aspects of Tolstoy's thinking, but also with Uspensky's *The Power of the Soil* in that both Hamsun and Uspensky made Mother Earth into something poetic, which gave its fruits to those who worked with the soil and were under its power. Like Uspensky, Hamsun believed that the peasantry had a mighty force in its possession, a force derived from the soil. The peasant also derived from the soil a wisdom and that higher truth which led to an earthly paradise.

However, there are great differences between the ideal of life visualized by Hamsun and Uspensky, and between their views on the fate of the peasant as part of the development of civilization as a whole. Hamsun called on the peasant to renounce his will and mind and to become merged completely with nature, to be meek, to reject civilization. He compared man to a tree, to a blade of grass and saw in the similarity the expression of the immutable and highest law of life. Long before *Juices of the Soil* appeared, Uspensky in *The Power of the Soil* compared the life of the peasant to the life of a blade of grass in the field. But Uspensky did not praise this life; on the contrary, he pointed to its limitations, to the disparity between this kind of a life and the high calling of a free man. Uspensky was also ready to curse civilization, but at the same time he showed that the peasant was also closely interested in the successes of civilization. Uspensky, too, knew the power of fatalism over the mind of the peasant, but he tirelessly sought for ways of freeing the peasant from the feeling of doom before nature. And one of the ways lay in collectivism and in the solidarity of the people. Uspensky remained a defender, not of peasant labor in general and not of the village community (*obshchina*) under serfdom and all types of authority, but of the free "large cooperative economy in which no one would go hungry, [and] in which the educated person would find a place..." (VII, p. 105).

A keen observer of the village of his time, Uspensky was forced to admit that it offered no conditions for a normal life. In order to live a humane life one would have to leave the village. Uspensky was grieved to see that all who were gifted and energetic had left the village and were trying to do so, not finding in it the opportunities to apply their strength and having lost the "appetite for peasant labor." Uspensky had to face the bitter truth that the intelligentsia was also afraid of the village, as well as the peasant and his needs.

Uspensky was one of the first in Russian and world literature to raise the question about the need to revitalize the individualistic psychology of the peasant. While fighting antihumanist attitudes toward the village, he did not idealize it, though at times he fell into poetic raptures about certain aspects of the life of his hero, Ivan Ermolaevich.

CHAPTER 5

Venus of Milo.
Vypryamila–*A Manifesto of Democratic Esthetics and Ethics*

> "...most often of all I go to the Louvre. That is where one can come to one's senses and get healthy again.... The best and holiest here is the Venus of Milo."

I *Uspensky in the Louvre*

DURING his stay in Western Europe in 1872 and 1875-76, Uspensky often visited the Louvre which he called the "great healer." "I go there nearly every day. It has its share of nonsense and abominations, but there is also much that is beautiful," he wrote (XIII, p. 112). According to Uspensky's own words and recollections by his contemporaries, the strongest impressions on Uspensky were made by the ancient statue of Venus of Milo.

What the statue meant to Uspensky was told in *Vypryamila* (*Straightened Out*) (subtitled "A Fragment from the Notes of Tyapushkin"–"Otryuki iz zapisok Tyapushkina") published in 1885–many years after Uspensky first saw the statue. His thoughts then were less clearly defined, though they reflected what Uspensky had long been interested in: questions of life, esthetics, and ethics. The most important effect the statue had on him was that it made him think about man and the society of his time.

To Uspensky, the creator of the sculpture was not interested primarily in showing Venus's "feminine charms" as "she is completely covered—one sees her face, chest, and part of her thighs." From the point of view of formal beauty the statue is not perfect. She is an "armless cripple," "a statue that is falling apart, with a damaged cheek and showing cracks from age...."

It was a far cry from other Venuses whose creators emphasized above all their feminine features which were what "first meet one's eyes." The Venus of Milo, noted Uspensky, was less "beautiful" than many contemporary Parisian women.

At one time the "destroyers of the beautiful"—the "nihilists" from the newspaper *Russkoe slovo*—wrote sarcastically about "Venus's thighs" and mocked those who admired the ancient statue. This vulgar nihilism was effectively refuted by Uspensky in *Vypryamila* (part of the cycle *Koy pro chto (A Little About Something)*. Uspensky knew, of course, that the creation of the sculpture involved great artistic skill, and that the beauty of the statue was revealed through physical form. Uspensky was not an ascetic, still, for him the beauty of the sculpture did not lie in its sensual qualities but in its human content, its harmony, natural nobility, wholeness, and the spiritual and physical strength it conveyed. Gorky noted in his letter to K. S. Lvova, the Soviet writer, that "Venus *vypryamila* [straightened out] Gleb Uspensky by the perfect simplicity of its forms."[1] And it was indeed so, though the question of how Venus "straightened out" Uspensky is a complex one.

When he first saw the statue in the Louvre in 1872, Uspensky felt that it was something healing, something that was the opposite of the abomination and nonsense which he found in the art of his time. This feeling remained with Uspensky for the rest of his life. In his letter of May 10, 1872 to his wife, Uspensky spoke about the holiness of the Venus of Milo and said further that he had also gone to the Palais du Luxembourg where he saw an exhibition of the latest works of art. There he met hundreds of Venuses—"naked women in various forms for old men." Uspensky went on: "I noticed that besides producing a certain impression they have no meaning; one covers herself with her hand, another lies on her stomach, a third sits cross-legged, a fourth lies on her back—in short, a heap." Uspensky concluded:

The closer you come to contemporary art, the worse it becomes: girls of about thirteen years of age and having the most naïve expression on their faces are shown whispering something into the Satyr's ear, probably something vulgar since he is smiling in the most vile, disgusting way. When I looked at all this abomination, the Venus of Milo suddenly became very dear to me. . . . What a contrast between such meaningless feminine bodies and her.... (XIII, p. 111)

Uspensky contrasted the beautiful, chaste, spiritually rich Venus of Milo—to whom the sick Heine came every morning and wept—to the new, meaningless, vulgar thirteen-year-old "Venuses."

As indicated earlier, the image of Venus of Milo appeared in Uspensky's imaginative works many years after he had first seen the statue. The reason for this, according to A. I. Ivanchin-Pisarev, was that Uspensky first needed to meet someone in real life—"someone of a higher order in whom high ideals are not separated from his physical being and are harmoniously united with his personal experience.... Uspensky met such a person in the 1880's. She was Vera Nikolaevna Figner...."[2]

In a sense this explanation is correct, if one remembers the great effect, both moral and esthetic, which Vera Figner's personality had on Uspensky, who worshipped her with religious fervor. For him Vera Figner, like German Lopatin, embodied the heroic qualities of the revolutionary and democratic intelligentsia of Russia. Ivanchin-Pisarev's explanation is also supported by what Uspensky said about Vera Figner in "Venus of Milo," an unfinished work which was the forerunner of *Vypryamila*. In it Uspensky called Vera Figner the living confirmation of the ideal of human personality ("I recalled Figner...."). Finally, one should keep in mind that in the 1880's the beautiful for Uspensky was organically linked with the heroic; the heroic was an embodiment of the beautiful.

But Ivanchin-Pisarev's explanation was not entirely right. The fact is that the meaning of the "stone riddle" was not immediately clear in Uspensky's mind. This is indicated by Uspensky's letter to his wife, cited above. At that time—in 1872—what Uspensky saw in Venus was the ideal mother, the ideal woman. She was someone "with a face deeply intelligent; the modest, courageous mother; in a word, the ideal woman who must exist in life..." (XIII, p. 111).

Ivanchin-Pisarev, in a chapter of his memoirs entitled "From the Life of Gleb Uspensky" showed a somewhat different Uspensky in front of the statue of Venus of Milo. He wrote:

Uspensky exclaimed "Look!" and came up to me and said almost in
a whisper, "See the line of the head, the neck, ... chest ... not a
shadow of a smile on the face ... nothing vulgar! It is obvious that
the artist wanted to show, not the charm of Venus, but the beauty
of the human soul which can be imbued with greatness, can be one
with it. ... In her, in this being, there is only the human in the
highest sense of this word.[3]

These feelings were close to those which Uspensky came to
express later, in 1885, because the scene at the Louvre, described
by Ivanchin-Pisarev, took place during Uspensky's second visit
to France in 1875-76. It is possible that on this visit Uspensky
saw Venus not so much as an ideal mother and woman, but as
the embodiment of human soul imbued with greatness. But it
seems that Ivanchin-Pisarev, when he wrote his memoirs in 1907
and 1914-15, was unconsciously influenced by what he knew
Uspensky had said in *Vypryamila* and had attributed to
Uspensky opinions which the writer expressed ten years later.

The point here is that in order to understand Uspensky's
views on the statue of Venus it is not enough to know about
Uspensky's feelings for Vera Figner. What is important is to trace
the change which took place in Uspensky's thinking between
1872 and 1885. One of the results of this change was the
realization by Uspensky that the beautiful was to be found not
only in selfless, revolutionary, and heroic service to the people,
but also in the everyday labor of the people if that labor could
cease to be strenuous and harsh, and become free.

II *Venus of Milo and Ivan Ermolaevich*

Uspensky came to consider Venus of Milo from the standpoint
of a writer only after he had met Ivan Ermolaevich, the hero
of his sketch cycle, *Peasant and Peasant Labor*. And his reason
for doing so was not only to lend a poetic quality to the description of the "aristocratic-peasant soul" of Ivan Ermolaevich,
but also to explain the human significance of his existence.

In the two first chapters of *Peasant and Peasant Labor*
Uspensky tells how Ivan Ermolaevich struggles all his life simply
to exist. At the beginning of the work, Uspensky expressed grief
and puzzlement over the fact that Ivan Ermolaevich, and many
like him, spent all their lives doing hard and strenuous work.

But suddenly something occurred which shed some light on peasant life and revealed its meaning. Uspensky once happened to overhear Ivan Ermolaevich lamenting over a calf which would not drink milk: "There he is! Just look at him, the cursed one. It makes one sick just to look at him!" Uspensky was struck by the dramatic tone—the tone of grief with which Ivan Ermolaevich spoke these words.

He was reminded of another incident which took place in 1876 in the Louvre near the statue of Venus of Milo. A Russian artist who accompanied Uspensky on the tour tried to prepare him for the meeting with the remarkable work. The artist bitterly rebuked the Russian poet, Afanasy Fet, "whose verses dedicated to Venus do not contain a single point that would even slightly suggest what there is in this Venus." The artist wanted to be sure that Uspensky would be able "to perceive at least a little of the beauty of this wonderful work." As they walked down the corridor leading to the statue with as much awe as if they were going to visit someone who was dying, suddenly the artist "stopped, his hands falling helplessly, and turning to me said in exactly the same dramatic tone used by Ivan Ermolaevich, 'Tell me, please, what does this look like? Just look, what they have done...'" (VII, p. 31).

It seems that the museum curators had decided to do something about the part of the statue that threatened to crumble. Thus, "on the left knee and on the nose either something had been smeared or some white paint had been applied, as a result of which the nose of Venus of Milo resembled that of a duck...." The artist was shocked by what he saw; his feelings were outraged by the renovated Venus. The same note of emotional outrage was in the voice of Ivan Ermolaevich when he could not make the young calf drink milk. Uspensky concluded that Ivan Ermolaevich "was grieved in almost the same way as the artist, that is, he was outraged by the calf in the depth of his imaginative needs" (VII, p. 32).

This discovery enabled Uspensky to understand the life of Ivan Ermolaevich, which earlier had appeared to him as nothing but senseless toil. In *From a Village Diary* Uspensky had described his spiritual torment caused by observing the absurdity of a peasant's life. In *Peasant and Peasant Labor* the author confessed that his "spiritual sore" began to heal after he discovered the artist in Ivan Ermolaevich, that he experienced "the most pleasant moments" by coming to know Ivan Ermolaevich, and that he was surprised at his own moral recovery. Now it seemed to Uspensky that Ivan Ermolaevich struggled not only to exist and pay taxes, but because the varied farm labor fulfilled all his mental needs. Ivan Ermolaevich derived full moral satisfaction and esthetic pleasure from the bustle about calves and ducks (he "admired" the oats, "adored" the colt, and so on).

We find that the main subjects of Uspensky's future work, *Vypryamila,* namely, the image of Venus of Milo and the criticism of Fet's well-known poem, appeared for the first time in his essay "The Poetry About Peasant Labor" ("Poeziya zemledelcheskogo truda") (1880) which is part of the sketch cycle *Peasant and Peasant Labor.* Here, however, Uspensky did not yet deal with the social, general, and humanistic significance of Venus of Milo. The stone being was treated as the embodiment of perfect beauty which inspired the highest esthetic emotions; such emotions, according to Uspensky, were experienced not only by the true artist, but also by the genuine peasant-worker. In *Peasant and Peasant Labor* the image of Venus of Milo is not the central theme, but serves to illustrate Uspensky's thoughts about the meaning of Ivan Ermolaevich's life and to bring out the inner world of the peasant-poet. Here, however, Uspensky did not explain in detail what he objected to in Fet's poem about the "stone riddle."

III   *"A Girl Student"—A Painting by N. A. Yaroshenko*

In Uspensky's cycle of sketches *Conversations with Friends . . .* (1883) we meet with a new character who also appeared later, somewhat modified, in *Vypryamila* (1885). The character was borrowed from a painting—"A Girl Student" ("Kursistka") by a friend of Uspensky's, N. A. Yaroshenko, who was one of the directors of the Association of Travelling Art Exhibits (*Tovarishchestvo peredvizhnykh khudozhestvennykh vystavok*). The first version of the painting was shown in March 1883 at the 11th Travelling Art Exhibit in St. Petersburg.[4] Uspensky used the character—a girl "aged fifteen or sixteen, a secondary-school or college student" who "runs with a book under her arm"—in describing his idea about the harmony of life based on peasant labor. The character appears in his essay "Concerning a Picture."

Yaroshenko's "girl student" was regarded by his contemporaries as the symbol of young Russia. No other Russian painter, except Repin, had created such a vivid, penetrating, and exciting portrait which succeeded in capturing the spirit of progressive Russian youth of the time. Yaroshenko may, indeed, be considered a chronicler in painting the epoch of revolutionary Populism. Besides "A Girl Student" he painted many other pictures including "The Prisoner," "G. I. Uspensky," "Student," "A Progressive Young Woman," "Near a Lithuanian Castle," and "Arrest of a Propagandist Girl."

To Uspensky, the most important thing about the painting was that "the graceful, the genuine, and the real—the fusing of the features of a young woman and a young man in one face, in one figure, showing not a feminine or masculine but a 'human' conception—immediately lighted up and gave meaning to the hat, the plaid, the book, and turned the picture into a new and bright human image, an image that was coming into being and that had never existed before" (VIII, pp. 166-67).

This interpretation of Yaroshenko's picture, portraying a new type of Russian woman, reflected the feelings of the progressive youth of the time. It should be noted that Yaroshenko, like Uspensky, was able to convey in his works the thoughts and feelings of the revolutionary Socialists of the time. These two "Populists"—one in literature and the other in painting—were more than friends; they shared a common social and moral outlook. This is reflected in Uspensky's penetrating comments on Yaroshenko's painting and in the fact that Uspensky served as the model for the staunch revolutionary locked in a stone cell in Yaroshenko's painting, "The Prisoner" (1878). Yaroshenko's portrait of Uspensky, done in 1884, succeeds in conveying the spiritual state of the writer, shown in a posture in which his friends often saw him: Sitting with his head bent and a cigarette in his hand. The expression of his eyes shows sorrow, questioning, and suffering. The gesture of his hands with long sensitive fingers suggests the mental suffering of the writer.[5]

The human thought which underlies the harmony embodied by the girl student in *Conversations with Friends . . .* acquires concrete social meaning in *Vypryamila* in which Uspensky

turned to the image of a severe type of young woman. About
her he wrote:

... the deep sorrow ... which was not her own sorrow and which
was shown on her face, in every movement of hers, was so harmoniously fused with her personal sorrow that the two sorrows
became one, and it was absolutely impossible to find in her heart,
soul, thought, even her dream anything that could diminish or destroy
the harmony of self-sacrifice, which she personified. ... (X₁, p. 251)

Here, in the image of the severe young woman an idea was
introduced that was shared by many revolutionaries of the
time, namely, the idea of the "harmony of self-sacrifice."

These two young women who embodied two types of harmony
aroused similar feelings in Protasov and Tyapushkin, the heroes
of *Conversations with Friends* ... and *Vypryamila,* respec-
tively. Stopping at an artist's studio, Protasov saw a small
painting and "suddenly he came to life, came to his senses, and
returned to a state of mental health and excellent memory...."
The severe-looking young woman evoked similarly strong and
happy impressions in Tyapushkin which were linked to Venus
of Milo. The important thing is that the harmony embodied by
the girl student made Protasov reflect on the harmony of peasant
labor. This transition from a picture to peasant life, which may
appear somewhat abrupt, is again found in *Vypryamila*. There
the "young woman of a severe, almost monastic type" appeared
immediately after the description of "an insignificant village
scene." Tyapushkin

was lost in thought as he looked at a village woman turning hay;
all of her, her whole figure with her skirt tucked up, her naked feet,
her red headdress, and the rake in her hand with which she threw
the dry hay from the right to the left, "lived," and not worked, lived
in such complete harmony with nature, the sun, the wind, the
hay, the whole landscape with which her body, her soul ... seemed
to merge, that I watched her for a long, long time, thought and felt
only one thing: "how good!" (X₁, pp. 250-51)

It is significant that the same feeling ("How good!," "How
glorious!",) was also inspired by the girl-revolutionary who
personified the "harmony of self-sacrifice" and by the girl
student.

Thus, we see that in Uspensky three related images began to take shape: the image of the beautiful in art (Venus of Milo and the "Girl Student"), the revolutionary, and the peasant and the village. They embody different types of harmony; they are expressions of the perfection of different aspects of human life and the human spirit.

The link between the story about Ivan Ermolaevich and *Conversations with Friends* ..., and *Vypryamila*, a work dealing with the ideal of beauty and its social meaning, constitutes one of the central points in Uspensky's outlook on life. In Uspensky, work, the heroic, and the beautiful became one indivisible whole.

IV   *Polemics Against Fet*

What has been said above touches only upon certain aspects of *Vypryamila*. To have a full understanding of the work it is necessary to consider the rise of political and ideological reaction in the 1880's, the artistic trends of those years, and the position which Uspensky occupied in the literary movement of the time.

As Uspensky noted, the apologists for the fashionable trend of "art for art's sake" saw the statue of Venus of Milo as the embodiment of the "pure" and the "eternal" which awakened "ecstasy," "a feeling of bliss," and delight in the "laughing body." Uspensky's treatment of the statue in *Vypryamila*, on the other hand, expressed the best hopes of the revolutionaries of the time. *Vypryamila* may indeed be considered a militant manifesto of democratic esthetics and ethics. It appeared at a time when there was a noticeable trend of turning away from the progressive ideas of the 1860's and 1870's. Many had written about the Venus of Milo, including Chateaubriand, Lamartine, Musset, Hugo, and Théophile Gautier. But in world literature, Uspensky gave the most profound social and ethical interpretation of this immortal work of art.

Vypryamila contains a sharp attack against the essay and poem by Fet on the statue of Venus of Milo.

In his *From Abroad* (1857) Fet described his visit to the Louvre and tried to show that the statue of Venus was a work of art and had no social significance and nothing to do with social struggle:

Let's go on. A great esthetic delight awaits us. At the end of one of the galleries there arises an image to which there is no equal in sculpture. Here we have the Venus of Milo. . . . Out of the clothes which fall to the thighs in a most charming curve blooms the body of the goddess with young, cold skin. This velvet, cool, and supple tendril of an early flower meets the first rays of the sun that has just broken through a thick cloud. No breath has touched it; the very dawn has not yet shed its happy tear on it. The goddess is not coquettish; she does not seek to please. The charming curve of her body is due to nothing else but the snakelike suppleness of her limbs.

She leans on her left foot; the lower part of the torso obeys the movement while the upper part seeks balance. Go around her; hold your breath and admire the inexpressible freshness of the figure and the virginlike, severe magnificence of the chest, which seems to compete for beauty with the somewhat pressed right hand and with this wonderful, supple, triangular fold of the skin which forms in the back under the right arm. Look at it from different angles, and you will see new curves, all most delicate and perfect. And look at this slightly tilted head turned somewhat to the left. When you are near it and look upward, it seems as if the hair, slightly curly and somewhat thrown back, was hastily gathered into a knot. But step back a little so that you can see the parting of the hair, and you will be convinced that it was the Graces that had parted the hair. Only they can be coquettish in so modest a way.

About the beauty of the face, how can anyone succeed in describing it? A proud consciousness of all-conquering power breathes in the very line of the lips and eyes, in the outline of the nostrils. But this pride is not the outgrowth of any convictions; such an outgrowth is always obtrusive and insulting to the eye, however skillfully it is hidden. This is an expression inherent in the very phenomenon. This is the pride of a beautiful horse, a mighty lion, a magnificent peacock, a flower in bloom. This has nothing to do with what the artist had been thinking. The artist did not exist; he had given all of himself to the goddess, to his Venus-the-Victorious. There is nothing in her eyes that suggests premeditated thought; everything that the marble statue freely sings to you is what the goddess herself says, and not the artist. Only such art is clean and holy; the rest is desecration of art. . . . When at the moment of ecstasy there arises before the artist an image smiling gratifyingly, an image which gently warms his bosom, filling his soul with sweet trepidation, then let him concentrate all his strength only on conveying that image in all its fullness and purity; sooner or later he will succeed. There can be no other aim in art . . . He who dares to add anything to this should be subjected to public scorn.[6]

We have quoted the above passage, summing up Fet's point of view, because it is so little known. Fet had finely observed and poetically described the outward appearance of the statue of Venus of Milo. Of course, the outward, physical beauty is there. But Fet paid attention only to this and had failed to note the "prophetic" social and moral strength conveyed by the statue. His reasoning, therefore, falls into esthetic Naturalism, and this approach angered Uspensky who felt that pure art and Naturalism were closely related to each other. Thus, his polemics against Fet were at the same time an attack against "pure art" which tended to deprive the statue of Venus of social and moral significance, and against Naturalism which sought out only physical beauty in the statue.

It is unlikely that Uspensky remembered exactly what Fet had said about the statue of Venus. It is possible, however, that in working on *Vypryamila* Uspensky read Fet's *From Abroad* and his poem on Venus printed in *Sovremennik*. It should be noted that Fet became known in the 1880's as the poet of the school of "pure art." His first collection of poems, *Evening Lights* (*Vechernie ogni*) was published in 1883, and another collection of poems by the same title came out in 1885, the same year as *Vypryamila*.

Uspensky said in *Vypryamila* that Fet understood nothing of the enormous impression produced by the statue of Venus of Milo. Fet did not even get to "cling to the edge" of it. Seduced by the "name" of Venus, Fet "recreated" only her feminine beauty and "forced what does not laugh—to laugh, what does not thrill— to thrill, what does not excite—to excite."

Fet's poem about the statue of Venus (1856) is, as follows:

> Both chaste and bold,
> Naked to the waist,
> Blossoms the divine body
> With everlasting beauty.
>
> Under this whimsical canopy
> Of slightly lifted hair,
> How much prideful bliss
> Pours out from the celestial face.

Thus, breathing passion,
Thrilled by the sea foam,
And fluttering with all-conquering power,
You look out in eternity.[7]

Commenting on Fet's poem, Uspensky said in *Vypryamila* that the artist who made the statue of Venus was not at all thinking of feminine beauty only. In Paris, Uspensky noted sarcastically, "one can find thousands of women who surpass Venus in beauty" (X, p. 269). The artist, said Uspensky, had a higher aim and, therefore, exposed only the upper part of Venus's body, so as not to lead the viewer to have banal thoughts about feminine beauty. In contrast to the statue of Venus were the fashionable modern sculptures of the time. "Whether these works depict 'beauty,' 'truth,' 'charity,' or 'despair'—they are all in the nude. You read in the catalogue: 'truth' but your eyes wander elsewhere.... 'Despair'...you come up to it and look and start thinking not at all of 'despair' but: 'Here's a woman...what a woman...spread like a white sturgeon'" (X₁, p. 269).

Uspensky's opinions on art were directed not only against Fet, but also against those, who in the 1880's considered the beautiful in art as the opposite to the life of the common people and to the heroic struggle of the intelligentsia. In this connection it is necessary to note the following circumstance:

Originally, Uspensky's essay cycle *In a Slipshod Manner* (1885) included an essay entitled "An Unfinished Chapter." It tells about a certain "little man" who visited Uspensky and started reading what the latter had written.

Hurrying from page to page he, I noticed, became excited about something which was obviously not very pleasant to him. He started throwing out whole pages without reading them and finally, without reading the manuscript to the end, put it down and cried, "No, this is awful!" And then he delivered a monologue about the "public" which is apparently disgusted with the cruel pictures of life with which it has so long been treated, and about art in general, about Pushkin, Shakespeare, Raphael. (X₁, pp. 480-81)

In answer to the chorus of such "little men" who adored Raphael and hated works about the peasant, Uspensky decided that he would stop writing in his usual manner. He combined the "Unfinished Chapter," which discusses the "suffocating gloom" of village life, with the "Notes of Tyapushkin" on the status of Venus of Milo, that is, with a subject which at first glance would seem to have nothing in common with the gloomy content of the "Unfinished Chapter" which so distressed the "little man." Actually, however, the story of Venus of Milo forms an essential part of Uspensky's writings and logically follows the "Unfinished Chapter," for it constitutes a generalization of Uspensky's esthetic and ethical views and his social ideal. It helps explain the meaning of his writings and is an answer to the advocates of "art for art's sake."

V Vypryamila

Tyapushkin began his notes with what the esthetes would consider a blasphemous assertion that the Venus of Milo— the image of "human essence"—stood for the same things as he himself, an ordinary and worn-out rural schoolteacher who lived in a freezing-cold hut. These were the same things which the great revolutionary principles of 1789 stood for. All three were to the same degree "unquestionable." They were different manifestations of the same line which

through the principles, through hundreds of other great phenomena, thanks to which man grows, will perhaps lead him to that perfection that will enable him to understand Venus of Milo. "And there, if you please are beauty and truth [in Venus of Milo], but here, you have only peasant bast shoes, torn sheepskin coats and fleas!" I beg your pardon! (X_1, p. 247)

In making Venus of Milo stand for the same goals as the principles of 1789, Uspensky did not idealize the principles, which to him embodied genuine humanism and were the banner of all progressive mankind.

To Uspensky, the Venus of Milo enabled one to "feel" the ideal, the perfection of social life which man must achieve through intellectual search and revolutionary struggle. The "mystery of the stone being" gave great happiness and joy. It straightened out the "crumpled-up human soul" and made man "feel the joy of being a human being" (X_1, pp. 265, 270). The creator of Venus of Milo "had to impress on the heart and mind of the people of his time, of all time, of all peoples forever, the

great beauty of human being ... to show ... all of us the possibility of being beautiful ..." (X₁, p. 270). The beautiful,
in Uspensky's view, should inspire such feelings and awaken
such thoughts that the common people would reject "vile
reality."

In Dostoevsky's *Demons,* Stepan Verkhovensky says that the
"base slave," "the stinking, lewd lackey," rising in struggle, cut
up the "divine image of the great ideal" embodied in the Sistine
Madonna.[8] N. K. Mikhaylovsky fully agreed: "I share ... [Verk-
hovensky's] indignation, but I also understand the slave, though,
of course, his moral and physical purity will not be achieved
in this way. But all the same, his movements are understandable."[9] Mikhaylovsky believed that the Venus of Milo would not
be appreciated by the oppressed masses. He had a rather shallow
understanding of the social nature of the sculpture and said that
it expressed the feelings, thoughts, and interests of the slave
owners only. In each curve of the body were concealed injustice
and insult to the slave. If the slave should understand the
statue, said Mikhaylovsky, the statue would suffer the fate of
the Column Vendôme.

Uspensky did not have the vulgar sociological approach that
placed the beautiful in opposition to the feelings of the masses
rising in rebellion. His esthetic views were also opposed to the
Utilitarianism of Pisarev, who did not understand the real,
objective links between true beauty and social struggle, between
the beautiful and service to the people. Pisarev was convinced
that the feeling of dissatisfaction with ugly society, a feeling
caused by the contemplation of the beautiful "cannot lead to
anything but fruitless suffering."[10] In *Vypryamila,* Uspensky said
that after seeing Venus of Milo he felt repelled by society
"which is harmful, bad, and bitter to live in." In this sense
the statue of Venus gave pain and sorrow, but Uspensky did not
think they were meaningless suffering and sorrow, or that they
were the only feelings inspired by the statue.

Venus of Milo, said Uspensky, enabled one to understand how
deeply man was insulted and humiliated in the existing social
and economic order. In this sense the statue made one think
about how to change society. Though the statue did not solve
such questions, it raised them and "paints in our imagination
endless possibilities of human perfection. ..." It awoke the

desire "to straighten out, to liberate today's crippled man
for ... the bright future. ..."

Such were the feelings experienced by Tyapushkin when he
visited the Louvre. After seeing the Venus of Milo he felt the
need to live an irreproachable life. He was deeply happy that
the "great artistic work strengthened his desire to go to the
'ignorant masses.'" In his work in the small remote village
covered with snow, Tyapushkin recalled the happy moments he
spent in the Louvre and the statue of Venus, and he felt
"straightened out" and ready to perform his duty. The statue
pointed to the ideal which served as his guide as he carried out
the practical work of serving the people.

The contrast between truth which "straightened out" man and
cruel reality which crippled man is the man theme of *Vypryamila*.

Uspensky presented, on the one hand, the ugly image of the
"white-skinned idol" with a cigar in the mouth, which symbolized
the might and the antihuman character of the rulers of the
world, their hostility to the beautiful, to art, and creative work,
and on the other hand, Venus of Milo which embodied the ideal
of a free, human personality. On the one hand, there was the
cruel, naked, degrading "truth" of money, strenuous toil, and
the "suppression of man in man," and on the other hand—the
"human truth." Man in a world of social injustice was like a
crumpled-up glove. But it was worth blowing into this glove,
which would then come to resemble a human hand. And so
it was with man. His soul was crumpled up by the ugliness of
society, but let him turn to Venus of Milo and he would
straighten out and experience joy and feel inspired to serve
the people. Tyapushkin felt that his soul languished in provincial
society; he felt as if a chunk of ice lay in his chest. But when he
recalled the Venus of Milo something warm moved in his heart,
and the warmth grew into a strong and happy flame.

Venus of Milo with "almost peasantlike locks of hair on the
sides of her forehead," the graceful peasant woman turning hay,
and the "severe" young woman who personified the "harmony of
self-sacrifice" all suggested to Uspensky the beautiful, the ideal
life, and the need to struggle in order to realize that ideal.

Thus, we see that Uspensky had a truly amazing conception.
He saw in Venus of Milo—who embodied a general, human
ideal—resemblances to the Russian peasant. He linked the

statue of Venus which had universal significance to a peasant
woman with a rake in her hands. He saw similarity between the
goddess of love possessing great moral strength and a Russian
revolutionary woman who personified the ideal of self-sacrifice.
Uspensky had found an original way of fusing the general with
the national, the beautiful with the heroic, and the artistic with
the labor of the people.

VI *Desecration of Beauty*

Uspensky took delight in labor, regarding it as a kind of play
of physical and spiritual strength. In his sketch "Laboring
Hands" ("Rabochieruki") (1887) he speaks about the difficult
life of those who do strenuous physical work and about man
turning into a beast of labor. However, Uspensky saw in labor
not only drudgery, but also the "living human soul." "You look
at man who is said to be a machine," he said, "but you don't
see a machine; you only feel the wounderful charm of a human
being" (X_1, p. 147). Uspensky was fascinated by three hundred
young women cleaning wool. They worked from four in the
morning to eight in the evening—for thirty kopecks—but they
were not exhausted by the work. In them Uspensky saw "so
much living feminine beauty, grace, youth, and the spirit of
play that the usual idea of the 'working woman' is lost in the
satisfaction of seeing such abundance of energy." This energy
was manifest in everything: in the song which was like the summer lightning that strikes powerfully and rapidly at one end
of the barn and dies away at the other end only to strike again
at that end and move on to another point; in the inborn ability
to make every little gesture of the hand a beautiful movement;
in the very work itself which came to lose its monotonous and
tedious character. This energy made Uspensky feel a desire
to live, a desire that was "happy and cheerful."

Pointing out the esthetic significance of the scene just
described, Uspensky again discussed his conception of the
beautiful. "How many works I have read in my time," he wrote

in which the author tried to charm me, the reader, with descriptions
of feminine beauty: he gathers some twenty female figures, and in
order to astound me without delay strips them, the poor ones, places
them near some small puddle, lays them out along the shores of

this muddy pond in utterly scandalous positions which seem to him desirable, without a twinge of remorse.... In short, they want to charm us in various ways with womanly beauty, but I cannot recall a single instance in which I received from such work any impression of life, of the joy of being alive ... any impression of beauty that heals the soul and says to the tormented men: "do not lose heart!" (X₂, pp. 148-49)

Being an artist, Uspensky was saddened by the fact that the abnormal social relations of his time had led to a distortion and coarsening of the beautiful and deprived the worker of the opportunity of experiencing real, wholesome beauty. And the situation would remain so, said Uspensky, until the human and the normal would be presented "in the real, unaffected form of true beauty" (IV, p. 120).

In an abnormal society the beautiful did not arouse joy but led to something just the opposite—low, dirty feelings, thoughts, and action. Tyapushkin described the visitors to the Louvre whose taste was corrupted by the Paris boulevards and who looked at the Venus of Milo from the point of view of seductive "feminine charm." In "Laboring Hands" Uspensky describes the obscene conversations between some wordly-wise persons about the young working women mentioned above. And this was not mere talk; it revealed the fate of many working women who were turned into "living commodities." Uspensky, as Gorky did after him, was greatly pained by the perversion and the desecration of beauty.

Of course, to believe that the ideal embodied in the statue of Venus had the power to heal, inspire, and transform people was also a kind of Romantic Utopia. But it was a Utopia that would release social energy, lead to the formation of high moral standards, and make man better. After discovering the strength contained in "his riddle" which healed man's soul, Uspensky did not try to evade unattractive reality by taking refuge in his ideal, just as earlier he did not take refuge in the "poetry of peasant labor." In both instances Uspensky's Utopia served Realistic art, helped him to cope with the tasks of exposing injustice and encouraging the search for truth. Thus, in *Vypryamila* and "Laboring Hands" ("Rabochieruki") the discussion about Venus of Milo—about the human ideal—like the descriptions of the beauty of the young working women, expressed Uspensky's loathing for all distorted and desecrated beauty, for all that debased man.

VII Uspensky's Conception of the Social Servant

The above discussion shows that in Uspensky's mind art was closely related to morality—the beautiful to the life of the people, to the struggle of the intelligentsia, and to work that served the people. Beginning with the 1870's Uspensky's main object as a writer was to transform his writings into social deeds, to be a propagandist through his writings of practical programs that would bring happiness to the working class. Thus, in the 1870's the question of what makes a social servant—someone who served the people—became an urgent one for Uspensky.

In Uspensky's view a writer was a social servant. It was not enough that the writer truthfully describes the life of the people. He must be "the true spiritual father who [awakens] the consciousness" of the masses (VI, p. 29). And then, said Uspensky in *Willy-Nilly*, the writer must inspire the readers to serve the people. He must create stimulating, powerful works that lift the soul and teach how "to dedicate one's life" to the happiness of others (IV, pp. 312, 315).

Uspensky himself, in the 1870's, did not merely declare his sympathy for the laboring masses and express grief over their sufferings. He also became a propagandist for the idea of serving the people through practical deeds. He rejected the bureaucratic approach and the self-importance of Russian officials; he also disapproved of those theoreticians and practitioners of self-perfection who sought to evade reality by cultivating comforting illusions.

Dostoevsky's famous speech, delivered at the Pushkin celebration in Moscow in 1880, was condemned by Uspensky because it called for an escape from life and total submission. Uspensky dealt with the subject in his articles: "Pushkin Celebration" ("Prazdnik Pushkina") and "The Secret" ("Sekret") (1880). In them, Uspensky at first expressed sympathy towards Dostoevsky's speech, but later he felt that Dostoevsky was trying to debunk the Russian revolutionary. The main point of Dostoevsky's speech was: "Be humble, proud man, work humbly in the fields of the people." But, to Uspensky, the demand of the time was not for escape, not for faith in some god, not for submission to evil, but for action and for creative men of action—men more energetic than those brought up on "Raster-yaeva Street" with its stifling, oppressive atmosphere.

In dealing with the question of what makes a social servant and in general, what makes a decent person, Uspensky looked to the Russian revolutionary as the model. To Uspensky, the word "intellectual" carried with it great responsibility. This meant that the intellectual must be a person of action and a fighter, and not a time-server pronouncing the necessity of "curling up in fear." In his letter to A. Salikovsky, one of the advocates of such an attitude toward life, Uspensky said that a genuine intellectual, convinced of the abnormality of existing conditions, "must demand change" and stand up for his convictions "despite demands of the surroundings," in "dissent against the surrounding circumstances and state of affairs" (XIV, p. 295). This conception of the intellectual showed the influence of the revolutionary liberation movement of the time and reflected the strong, as well as the weak side of this movement both in terms of theory and practice.

Uspensky believed that the new intellectual *raznochintsy* who had freed themselves from the path of slavery and dedicated themselves to the people's well-being should be able to conquer evil and bring about healthy relations between men. In his works of the 1870's Uspensky created many characters who were intellectual fighters against injustice. They include the teacher Abrikosova ("The Incurable"—"Neizlechimy"), the youth Fedya ("From Notes of a Little Man"), Dolbezhikov ("No Resurrection"), the "foreigner" ("Three Letters"), a humanist (*Willy-Nilly*), and Fedusha ("Hungry Death"—"Golodnaya smert'"). They all experienced the need "to uphold the cause of the people, to sacrifice themselves, to bring happiness to the people in order to be happy themselves," to live for others instead of for "one's own nook" and "one's own stomach." The hero of "Three Letters" pointed out that it was necessary to turn one's sympathy for the people into action that served the people. "The worm of love for a man's close ones" ate through the heart and "shows that passive sympathy is not the whole truth." This thought, independently expressed here by Uspensky, and echoing Populist altruistic theories, is one of the basic ideas in his works.

In calling on his readers to serve the people, Uspensky sounded a heroic, militant note. In the story "She Gave Her Life for the Course" (1879) and in the notes "In Expectation of Something Better" (1883) Uspensky described two ways of working for the people's well-being: the "lawful" ways and the "unlawful" ways, the straightforward way and the zig-zag way. "Lawful" actions, that is, actions from above, actions carried out with the help of the state apparatus, did not lead to the people's well-being, but to a caricature of it.

To Uspensky the act of serving the people was not only a heroic and social act (let us recall his words: "It is necessary to act and act directly!"), but also a moral act. In *Willy-Nilly* Uspensky calls for acceptance of this new moral attitude, which reflected the attitude of the revolutionaries of his time. Uspensky's moral outlook, like his esthetic views, was formed in the heroic decades. To serve the people with one's heart and sword was a real source of happiness for man. It freed him from "beastly" instincts—from the philosophy in which the idea of " 'what's mine' and 'what's not mine' were predominant"—and enabled him to live a fuller life (VI, pp. 24-26).

In 1876 Uspensky expressed the important idea that work for others should be a person's aim all his life, and that such work was the source of happiness. He pointed out some of the characteristics of his heroes mentioned above: First of all, they had unity of word and deed; they rejected the abstract, bookish conception of life and of the needs of the people. To them, serving the people was not an amusement, or a temporary experiment, or an obligation, or "excursions among the people," or the expiation of sins, but an inner and constant need. Finally, their action was based on knowledge of people's life. Real work for real justice in human relations—this demand by Uspensky in some ways resembled the narrow stand of the liberals. Actually, it rested on profound philosophical and moral principles.

In contrast to those who served the people by practical deeds were the advocates of a perverted altruism, which was nurtured by the centuries-old system of serfdom which Uspensky called "inhuman reality" (*Willy-Nilly*). This altruism consisted in a lifeless, bookish, abstract devotion to lofty ideas, ignorance of real life, refusal to understand the real needs of the people, inability to satisfy these needs, and helplessness before them.

What Uspensky sought were conditions that would allow the all-round development of one's personality, which in turn would enable one to carry out conscious, active, and fruitful social deeds. In "Willy-Nilly," Uspensky discussed the basic ethical demand for those who wished to serve the people. Tyapushkin—who also appears in this work—found that only in performing social deeds, only in doing what was useful to the people could he "satisfy the needs of his personality." Only such work could develop one's personality and give one moral satisfaction. But such work, warned Uspensky, was not easy, for it demanded the ability not to become easily frightened or disillusioned; not to be lost in a real, living situation as opposed to an artificial situation; not to become confused when dealing with problems encountered by the people which were not general, abstract problems but the living, everyday problems of an Ivan, Matryona, and Sidor.

Those who undertake such work must possess a certain character formed in a school different from that of Tyapushkin. Thus, in "Willy-Nilly" Uspensky thought of contrasting Tyapushkin with persons of will who derived their intellectual strength and strength for action not from abstract conceptions of duty, but from living reality. Uspensky, however, failed to convert his thoughts into action, though his admiration for such persons of great will as Lopatin and Vera Figner clearly indicated that for him the highest manifestation of intellectual beauty, the ideal of human personality and the social service were exemplified by the Russian revolutionaries of the Socialist *raznochintsy* movement. At the same time, Uspensky was aware that the revolutionaries of his time had suffered bitter defeat and that the forming of active and energetic men from among the people would be a slow process, a process that had only just begun. Uspensky had thus far been unable to exert any noticeable influence on the life of his time.

Uspensky's search for positive, active persons from among the people was accompanied by much doubt, feelings of uncertainty, and contradictory thoughts. In his conception of the social servant, another tendency can be detected in addition to the one already described, also characteristic of Uspensky's thinking at this time. He had Utopian ideas about how to achieve the people's well-being, about how to build a life based

on collectivism, humanity, reason, and integrity, and about the
kinds of persons who could carry out this task. In the 1880's,
Uspensky observed with growing anxiety how the principle of
"what's mine" and "what's yours" was undermining fraternal
solidarity among people, influencing their psychology and their
actions more and more, and beginning to control the entire
social mechanism. Uspensky had described such a life as sinful.
In his last years, as in his essay, "By the Labor of One's Own
Hands," Uspensky sometimes talked about a life without sin,
"the truth of god" or "divine justice" without, of course, putting
any formal religious meaning into the terms.

Despite his skeptical attitude toward fantasizing about "what
and how things should be, what is just and how to be just,"
Uspensky often dreamed about and lamented the absence of
a "godly life." By this he meant a free, untrammelled life, a harmonious development of personality, fraternal solidarity of the
people, triumph of the beautiful, and happiness of the working
masses.

According to Uspensky's Utopian views, the duty of an intellectual was to replace the sinful life of bourgeois society with
"divine justice" (VIII, p. 84). Thus, in the 1880's Uspensky
regarded "him who served the people," that is, the social servant, as a type of "saint" who did not shun terrestrial questions
and did not seclude himself in caves and forests, preoccupied
with his own saintliness, but lived among the people and was
a "terrestrial worker" (VIII, p. 36). Uspensky devoted a whole
cycle of sketches: "The Blind Singer" ("Slepoy pevets") (1889);
"Rodion the Concerned," ("Rodion-radetel',") (1889); "Sensitive
Heart," ("Chutkoe serdtse") (1891); "Invisible Avdotya,"
("Nevidimka Avdotya") (1880) under the general title: *The
Invisible Ones (Nevidimki)*, to the portrayal of those "who
served the people"—"good people," "the invisible ones with big
hearts"—who dedicated their lives to the well-being of the people.

Of course, Uspensky's conception of the social servant who
was armed with love for the people, sensitiveness to others'
sufferings, good deeds, appeal to the conscience, moral purity,
and Christ's teaching about the brotherhood of men was Utopian
in nature. But the conception, though Utopian, was part of the
democratic movement of the time and thus had a positive significance. Uspensky turned not to those selected heroes whose

duty was to save the world, but to the common people from among the working masses and the intellectual *raznochintsy*. Discussing the inconspicuous but important work done by these people, Uspensky condemned the contemptuous attitude toward social questions and social activity on the part of those intellectuals who in the 1880's became disillusioned with struggle, ceased to care about the people's welfare, and abandoned the heroic ideas of the 1860's and 1870's ("A Good Russian Type" —"Khoroshy russky tip"), (1885). In the 1880's, Uspensky, for all his vacillations and contradictions, remained faithful to the militant "legacy of the sixties."

CHAPTER 6

The Power of Capital in Russia

> *"As earlier I was interested in the power of the soil—that is, the conditions of life of the working people, its evils and its goodness— I am now anxious to write a series of essays to be called 'The Power of Capital.'"*

USPENSKY'S works of the last period (1886-1893) show no diminution of intellectual vigor or social concern. In them he turned to the question of development of capitalism in Russia, displayed keen interest in the proletariat in Russian towns and villages, in Marxism, in the struggle of the proletariat in Russia and other countries, and continued to study the various forms of struggle of the peasants for land.

Immediately after completing *The Power of the Soil* and *Conversations with Friends* ... Uspensky, disillusioned with the "brutal" village, ran away from it—the source where he had earlier hoped to find the truth that would save society. In 1883 he left for the Caucasus. From that time on, until he became ill toward the end of his life, he was constantly going from one place to another in Russia. He was in Siberia, Bashkiria, on the Black Sea coast, on the Volga, the Sheksna River, and in various parts of Southern Russia.

I Migrant Russia. New Artistic Principles

In the 1880's Uspensky's interest began to shift from the independent peasant who lived by the labor of his own hands to the millions of farm laborers and migrant workers—the "landless farmers"—people who were exhausted by work and suffering from hunger, who went from one place to another in search of work. This shift of interest to the toiling masses marked a big stride forward for Uspensky. It meant that he did not stop at

the ideals which he worked out on the basis of the life of Ivan
Ermolaevich. As part of the Russian peasantry was driven off
the land, Uspensky turned to the tormenting and unfamiliar path
which alone could lead to the liberation of the working masses.
Many of them left their homes in the villages where they had
always lived and began to wander all over the Russian Empire
in search of bread, work, shelter, and land. In the 1880's nearly
thirty per cent of Russia's peasantry left their homes.

Among Uspensky's papers is a sheet on which was written
the title of a future essay, "The Working Tramps."

The phenomenon of migrant Russia brought about an important change in Uspensky's outlook on life, as well as in the
subject, tone, and structure of his works, and in his methods
of typification. In his works of the preceding period, the main
characters are the peasant and the author-narrator. Thus, for
example, Uspensky established the typical features of Ivan
Ermolaevich and Ivan Bosykh by tracing the logic of their
reasoning, and analyzing their character in terms of their relationship to the land, their families, the routines of peasant labor,
various conceptions of the "world" (*mir*) of the village, urban
civilization, and so on. Particularly important was the relationship between the hero-peasant and the author-narrator who had
Populist views and who tried to understand village life, but had
failed to exert any influence on Ivan Ermolaevich, to convince
him of the need to build another kind of life. Underlying the
descriptions of the relationship between the peasant and the
intellectual Socialist, a relationship which was complex and in
the final analysis fruitless, were those ideas which linked Uspensky to the Populists—to "peasant socialism."

Completely different ideas are found in Uspensky's cycles of
essays of the last period, including *A Letter from a Journey,
In a Slipshod Manner,* and *Visits to the Migrants.* In the version
of *In a Slipshod Manner* published in a journal, Uspensky
defined the characteristics of his new essays. Life, said Uspensky, went forward, but with such "unnecessary, absurd, and
cruel fortuitousness and complications that the expression 'in
a slipshod manner' with which I wish to describe this stupid,
difficult movement can perhaps only be mildly reproached...."
But since life was such, "the thought of the observer cannot
but also emerge somehow...in a slipshod manner," and this

in turn could not "but leave an imprint on the style and methods of literary composition." The essays, therefore, inevitably appeared disorderly, in which "topics were thrown together, and one speech is interrupted by another which is interrupted by a third, and so on." Uspensky asked the reader not to become confused by the *"apparent disorder"* of his observations, noting that despite their seeming disorderliness, the essays have a center in the same way as there was a center in life which "goes forward, goes toward truth, toward the triumph of truth . . ." (IX, pp. 595-96).

Underlying Uspensky's ideas about art in this last period was a desire to depict the migrant masses—the roaming, restless, and often embittered multitudes—in various conditions of their unstable life. And Uspensky, the author, roamed with them. What Uspensky described this time are not individual characters and scenes, but the masses, "mass dialogue," and mass scenes. In these descriptions may be seen Uspenky's new methods of typification.

Uspensky tried to understand the means by which the millions of migrants lived, and how they explained their bitter life. Hence, his persistent interest in what they said and how they said it. Uspensky particularly valued words spoken without restraint by the people, words not intended to be heard by the authorities, words that came from their suffering heart. Gorky once said that Uspensky "could not reproduce exactly the talk of the peasant because of tsarist censorship."[1] But Uspensky had succeeded in creating an amazing art—the "mass dialogue"—which reproduced the speech of the ordinary people and enabled Uspensky to overcome censorship.

Let us take, for example, the essay "So Far" (1887) from the cycle, *We, in Our Words, Dreams, and in Reality*. The essay was about an actual, but hardly poetic incident—the issuance of a circular about "cooks' children." The Minister of Education I. G. Delyanov, had issued an order forbidding the admission to gymnasiums of "children of coachmen, laundresses, small shopkeepers, etc." (1887). Uspensky gave a broad, general interpretation of the incident and used an original and effective, but extremely difficult form, that of "mass dialogue" with its meaningful pauses and hints, and expressive speech of the people.

Through the speeches, gestures, and manners of the people

Uspensky conveyed their extreme bitterness—sometimes concealed by humor—and their desire to express this bitterness and to discuss their situation. Uspensky found that the people's speech had an originality, which was inaccessible to the "clean public," that made it perfectly fluent and expressive, especially in cases where they talked among themselves. This quality of people's speech was particularly interesting and important for Uspensky, the writer, for it meant that the material presented by the life of the migrants contained the thoughts of the people expressed freely and fluently. Uspensky's object was to understand this thought and hear these words, make comprehensive comments on them, and sometimes to participate in the people's discussions and to guide them.

The changeable, unfixed psychology of the masses, their songs and laughter, talks and rumors about the urgent questions of life, happy hopes and real hardships, struggle against hunger and death on the road is all powerfully described by Uspensky. No other Russian writer of the nineteenth century before Uspensky had dealt with the life of the toiling masses. Uspensky now had little desire to stand before the suffering masses in his former role of the propagandist for a "sinless life" based on labor of one's own hands with the soil, even though at times he felt tempted to do so. The rumble of bitterness arising from the people told Uspensky the truth about life in the country and helped him understand and depict those processes which were taking place in the heart of postreform Russia, and leading to the 1905 Revolution.

The worn-out peasant, Uspensky admitted, "has no chance whatever of remaining in his old home"; "he is obviously fed up with it" (IX, p. 276). In "Unusual Situation" (1887), Uspensky described the gathering in Kakhov of millions of farm laborers—this "living commodity"—and said that "a real, desperate proletariat" was born.

In the preceding period, Uspensky told the story of the peasant's dependence on the soil, on the "slenderest blade of grass." In the second half of the 1880's he described the tragedy of the ever-growing power of money over the peasant. Uspensky, of course, could not have known that the stratification of the peasantry and the emergence of a rural proletariat were natural and inevitable, but he persistently showed what had destroyed the

peasant and had torn him away from the soil. Uspensky began
to look at life from the point of view of the homeless wanderer,
of the peasant driven away from the village by "infernal need."
Whereas Uspensky regarded the peasant-proprietor with scorn
and pain, his attitude toward the peasant-migrant and the farm
laborer was one of sympathy and concern. He was seized by
a feeling of helplessness and despair at the sight of the homeless toiling masses suffering from hunger and poverty, finding
themselves in the tenacious claws of capitalism which bought
the "living commodity."

"It's terrible, it's terrible, my dear brother, to go into the
world to earn pennies for bread. There's the world, all four
sides of it, and there's no end to it. Go! and find a ten-kopek
piece! . . . No, may God spare even the worst enemy such a fate,"
said the peasant Mikhaylo who had seen a good deal in his
time (in the story "The Small Dilapidated Hut," X_1, p. 142).
Sorrow for such people, the wish to find a way out for them,
somehow to make their life easier—these were the feelings that
guided Uspensky as he described in many of his essays and
sketches the "waves of people" roaming from one end of Russia
to another in search of "precious bread."

The meaning of this social and economic displacement in the
country was shown in "Rich Peasants" (1890), in which Uspensky used the same images with which several years before he
had described the poetry of farm labor and the power of the
soil. Now, however, under conditions of widespread dislocation
of peasants, these images acquired an entirely different meaning. The soil was at one time the mother that fed the peasant.
Now it was worked by the farm laborer who was made landless
by the landowner and the kulak, and land had become the
private possession of the well-to-do. The peasant, said Uspensky,
at one time went "to the wide steppe with the scythe, and
derived satisfaction from the work he did."[2] But times had
changed. Now the mower was no longer needed, as hay was
cut by some "mysterious monster, some powerful force [machine]
called Eruslanov,"[3] for which the steppe itself appeared like a
child's palm and the mower merely a helpless fly.

Due to these new conditions, Uspensky used new artistic
images to express his feelings of grief. The fields, cut by machines,
reminded him of two pictures by the Russian painter, Vasily

V. Vereshchagin. One shows a battlefield strewn with rows of dead bodies; another shows heaps of dead bodies.[4] In the steppe "the ears of cereal are scattered about like dead bodies." The mowing machine had "a long row of crocodilelike teeth which chew on the ear about which it has been so wonderfully said in a song: 'Grass appears in the field, the ear grows; it will ripen and dress itself in golden cloth. . . .'" But now Uspensky saw the "cut ears of wheat." "All the poetry of the farmland" was destroyed and trampled on without mercy. Mikula Selyaninovich,[5] looking at the "power of the soil" shattered by the machine, began to feel as if his own strength were being shattered (XII, pp. 234 ff.).

The writer's whole poetry was now created by considering the basic task: to show the processes of the development of capitalism in the country, the ruin of the peasant masses, their despair—beginning after the peasant reforms of 1861—their moral awakening, and the flare-ups of their anger and spontaneous protests.

For example, in the cycle of sketches entitled *Grekhi tyazhkie* (*Heavy Sins*) (1888), the triumphant march of the "sinner coupon" through Russia is described this way:

Just as soon as the sinner coupon, with its anti-christ stamp, touches a quiet rural station, a quiet village in the black earth zone, or a quiet river, and this touch is imprinted by throwing up a ship dock on the quiet river and a railway station or terminal in the free steppe—from that moment on, both at the station and in the village something starts going on that had never happened before; something that is not known by anyone, and most importantly, something that no one can help obeying. Some kind of an invisible force is breaking up the comfortable little houses engulfed by green poplar trees and building huge houses on the order of those found in the capital. One building after another is being built, without rest or stop; these buildings are made into hotels, huge stores never before seen here, from which crawl people formerly dressed simply, but now—as if the clothes had put themselves on—in new, fantastic suits, jackets, morning coats, all sorts of unusual hats and bustles. This unknown force, not saying a single word . . . begins to drive out the peaceful inhabitants—who used to spend quiet summer evenings playing cards —to chanson cafés, to country gardens, force them to listen to chansonettes in an incomprehensible language, teaches them not to be ashamed of wearing short skirts above the knee nor of the suggestive movements of circus acrobats and riders. And immediately, as if by magic, it hypnotizes great numbers of modest and completely innocent maidens—daughters of local, not rich, residents, chasing them out to a new trade on a new sidewalk. Yesterday one of these innocent girls decided to marry the deacon's son or the clerk in a vegetable store who makes three rubles. Another one was ready to sell pretzels, a third one and her friend had almost decided to enter a convent. But the anti-christ came, amazed them with thousands of unexpected things, interrupted and destroyed all the ideas that they had when they were being brought up in a way of life in their quiet family, in a quiet village that had existed from time immemorial. And he left them without any thoughts, but "implanted" fear and "disaster" in those who had nothing. He mocked their simple homemade dress, mocked their naïve hopes of becoming happy with a clerk or the deacon's son, and dragged them out—almost without resistance—as if they were guilty of being ignorant and poor, to gardens, cafés, outdoor festivals, and hotel rooms. He enslaved them with clothing, hats, umbrellas, and high-heeled shoes.

This mark of the anti-christ and its consequences in the quiet corners of the Russian land were for the most part welcomed by people who did not care about themselves and the near future. They welcomed them as happy events—as a beneficial rain which waters desert places and awakens life in them. But whoever had a drop of feeling, so that he could sense the difference between "honey and tar" . . . and good and evil—this person could not, without feeling a terrible grief, indifferently look on at all this sudden, instant prosperity in our quiet villages. . . . (XI, 403-4)

The writer found himself in one of these former patriarchal Cossack villages. It had turned into a town in the steppes which was

already marked by the anti-christ to be along the route of the Novorossiysk railway. And through the station of Tikhoretsky it was already welded by the iron embrace of rails to all of Russia, and through the Black Sea and the port of Novorossiysk—with the whole wide world. It was already stuck to the whole wide world, and the wide world was stuck to it. And they are already greedily drinking "fresh blood" from one another. . . . The city "prospered"— not by the day, but by the hour—and kept growing, kept being painted, began to be like a dandy in every respect—and the common people flocked here by the thousands. . . . (XI, 406, 408)

Here, there is an entire, well thought out series of artistic, figurative devices forming an agitated, journalistically revealing

—and at the same time—metaphoric style of the writer. Not only socio-economic processes are reflected here, but also the feelings of the author himself—his grief, his fears for the fate of man. This style can be characterized as lyricism in prose.

Another example is his use of symbolism, also prompted by the life of the common people: In the eighties of the last century, an immigrant muzhik appeared in Russia with a "microscopic horse" and a "microscopic carriage." The writer was astonished at the sackcloth covering the cart, "haphazardly made of tree branches." Here is how Uspensky described this sackcloth:

It all consisted of patches, sewn together, one patch sewn on another . . . this was the labor of great-great-grandmothers, given to great-grandmothers as cast-off clothing. They gave the remains of the cast-off clothing, after doing some work on it, to the grandmothers; and the grandmothers, having redarned and resewn all these patches of preceding generations, gave them to their granddaughters. And this entire chronicle of untiring and unending work is now going [on the cart] somewhere into an unfamiliar distance, protecting [someone] from the rain and the sun, not holding a promise of anything but the same kind of a continuation of the same kind of untiring labor.

In the author's imagination, the sackcloth covering became a certain symbol: each of its threads spoke of "labor from one century to the next." He pictured heavy labor in the harvesting of the flax, its processing until it became thread, material, a shirt, and finally, a patch. The sackcloth cover forced Gleb Uspensky to depict to himself and to his reader the sleepless nights of spinning, weaving, and sewing. And all this, in his imagination, was done only so that the nakedness of the poverty-stricken workers would be covered. And at the end of these "centuries of labor," said the liberal writer, nothing turned up except for the unresolved question: "And what do they live for?" (IX, pp. 257-58).

Uspensky was deeply pained by what he saw: he regarded the impoverishment of the masses and the displacement of the peasant as a personal tragedy, and as the tragic death of the poetry of farm labor. But saddened as he was, Uspensky did not cease thinking about the fate of the toiling masses in Russia. He did not ignore the universal and historical fact that new conditions of life and work had caused yesterday's peasant to

think and had turned him into a wage worker. This had already
been observed by Uspensky, in the 1870's ("Checkbook," "Bad
News," "Living Country"). The idea was expanded in 1883 in
a series of sketches entitled *Travel Notes* based on Uspensky's
trips to the Caucasus. Acknowledging the victory of capital
even in the most remote regions of Russia, Uspensky, in *Travel
Notes*, mocks his own illusions about the villages and tries to
examine the causes for the widespread unrest among the workers in Baku ("Bloody Battle"—"Poboishche"). He strives to reveal
and explain the sources of the punctiliousness of the worker when
a question arose concerning his personality or his dignity as a
human being. Uspensky was led to an important conclusion; he
returned to the thoughts which he first expressed in "Checkbook" and in "Bad News."

Also important in this respect is the sketch "Harvest" ("Urozhay") (1886). Speaking of the millions of migrant workers,
Uspensky pointed out that the "people's roaming"—something
that had not happened in the entire period of serfdom—had great
social and moral significance. He talked about the moral and
educational impact resulting from the mass exodus from the
village-ghetto. "The peasant under serfdom," wrote Uspensky,
"chained to his place by the power of the landowner, would
have had no idea of what the peasant torn away from his traditional place would run into..." (X_1, p. 62). The wandering
peasant, said Uspensky, came to suffer much, to think things
over and find out what goes on in the world. The new situation
enriched his thinking by making him understand things about
the contemporary way of life that he would never have dreamed.
There was much the migrant workers learned. They came to
know life "in its real form," to learn about the bosses as they
really were. Uspensky noted that this knowledge would not
leave the workers with happy thoughts; it would only make
them bitter: there would be "bitter language, bitter sneers, impu-
dence, rudeness," the desire "to hit back" at the first opportunity
(X_1, p. 64). Uspensky spoke of the "violent forms" of awakening and of the first outbreak of anger in the working man.

II   *The Reign of Capitalism*

It is not surprising that we find Uspensky in 1884 searching
for a "completely new way that would have nothing to do with

Populism." "In this field," he said, "I have done all I could do, and I have now come to a point of pouring from one empty vessel to another empty vessel" (XIII, p. 403). In his letter to V. Sobolevsky in late 1887 and to V. Goltsev in 1888, Uspensky told about his plans for new works that would deal with the power of capital. The new theme filled him with enthusiasm, he said, and he emphasized its importance for understanding Russian life. He realized that the development of capitalism in Russia was certain and inevitable, but he also saw that this development would have frightful consequences. This view is reflected in the artistic methods of depicting the new system and the people under it. While acknowledging that capitalism had brought with it something positive—it made the working people think, broke up the system of serfdom, and encouraged the feeling of individuality—Uspensky rejected the negative aspects of its development. In the second half of the 1880's he concentrated his attention on the destructive forces of capitalism.

In describing the bloodthirsty, predatory aspect of capitalism, its opposition to the well-being of the people and to the beautiful, Uspensky resorted to caricature and the grotesque, which resemble the sketches of Maxim Gorky and the satires of Vladimir Mayakovsky, Alexander Serafimovich, Ivan Bunin, and Alexander Kuprin. The relationship between the capitalist system and the people, said Uspensky, was one of sale and purchase, a matter of cold calculation. The hero of the new life could buy everything: somebody else's wife, ballet dancer, authority, and votes. There were no other kinds of social and moral ties under capitalism. The bourgeoisie reminded Uspensky of something putrid, cold, swollen, and stinking, while the bourgeois way of life could be summed up in the words: "baseness of moral motives" ("The Bourgeois"—"Burzhuy").

Uspensky saw the bourgeoisie as the "belly" and capitalism as the "voluptuous mouth" champing "tender pieces of meat" and drinking "fresh blood from virgin places"(*A Letter from a Journey*). The capitalist sinner "litters" the virgin places—the "clean," "virgin soil"—bringing with it "dirt and all kinds of filth." There was something deeply offensive about society based on money. The actions of the new masters of Russia were oppressive. The well-being of a man under capitalism was built on the bones of the toiling masses ("After the Feast").

The activity of the factory owner and merchant, Ivan Kuzmich Myasnikov, had something "resembling ravage, disappearance, the death of something" ("Checkbook"). Capitalism introduced into all spheres of life "boredom, dryness, pettiness, and dullness" and "anxiety over pennies" ("Petty Agents of Large Enterprises"—"Melkie agenty krupaykh predprivatey"). The debasement of man was what the bourgeois system led to.

Uspensky's views concerning the moral and esthetic, the emotional and psychological aspects of capitalism were linked with ideas about innocent peasant democracy, with Utopian socialism, the Enlightenment, and the teaching of the Russian revolutionary democrats about human nature. Uspensky approached capitalism not from the point of view of the industrial proletariat, but of the independent peasant of the 1870's and of the village proletariat or semi-proletariat. These were the farm laborers or city laborers of the 1880's, millions of whom, due to the development of capitalism, had left the village to taste the sweetness of wage labor, and had come to know from personal experience the reigning capitalist order with its innumerable bosses. They led a homeless and half-starved existence, pondered over their situation, but still had not abandoned their vain hopes of returning to the village and the soil, and living an independent life. The feelings and moods of the people torn away from the soil—yesterday's peasants—who suffered much from the development of capitalism in Russia, were expressed in Uspensky's works of the last period.

Uspensky was filled with anxiety as he watched man being trampled on by machine. In his horror and sorrow before the inhuman ways of capital, Uspensky was close to N. Mikhaylovsky and other Populists who were particularly distressed by the crippling and suffering of man in their time. Uspensky differed from the Populists, however, in that his descriptions of capitalism revealed not only fear and horror, but also the desire to understand the nature of capitalism and its impact on the fate of man, its characteristics under Russian conditions, and its influence on the thoughts and actions of the working masses.

While not ignoring the fact that capitalism was established from above, that is, by the autocratic government, Uspensky was interested mainly in its development below, that is, how it affected the people, in particular, the peasantry. This approach to the process of capitalism excluded consideration of its accidental quality and its instability. Uspensky, therefore, thought about the theme of the "power of capital" and the "power of the machine" in the same way as the "power of the soil," and emphasized the normalcy and strength of the developmental processes of capitalism in Russia.

He described various aspects of the breaking-up of the economic base of peasant life under the new conditions. He made comparisons between the regions already affected by capitalist development and regions yet unaffected by it; between pre-reform towns and towns based "on the ruble" ("People of All Ranks"); between patriarchal peasant customs and bourgeois domestic life. He portrayed the kulak and his way of life. He described the primitive factory and the factory "refined by humanity and philanthropy." The range of subjects Uspensky dealt with is broad; they include the railway boom and the good effects of the Siberian railway; the activities of banks and joint-stock companies; the traditional economic ties between Russian and foreign firms; the "old-fashioned" capital of merchants and the latest invention—the checkbook; the Cuban plantations which were technically well-equipped and organized on the American pattern and, in contrast to it, primitive peasant economy with its chief tool, the wooden plow; capitalist activities on the Russian rivers; Russian economic conditions and international politics; the rivalry between Russian and foreign capital; and economics and war.

The development of capitalism also changed the landscape of Russia. Uspensky noted this very subtly. His landscape sketches, as a rule, are meager and do not have a meaning by themselves alone. They are always woven into a description of the economic life or the mood of the masses, and are connected with his own thoughts on the "evil of the day."

In this connection, his descriptions of the Sheksna River in *Sketches of a Changing Time* (*Ocherki perekhodnogo vremeni*) (1887-1890) are significant. Notwithstanding its swiftness, force, and picturesqueness, for some reason this river seemed uninteresting to the author. He decided to find an explanation to the riddle. His research of the question brought him to that "dark place" in any Russian newspaper of that time, where the value of the ruble, stock market prices, and so on, were given in the smallest print. And everything that was then occurring on the Sheksna River suddenly became clear to the writer—just due to those numbers. The commercial "tendentiousness" of the river was the source of the tedium that engulfed him. He sees "a mass of haystacks, crowded in hundreds at the very edge of the riverbank, huddled closely, tightly, like a regiment of soldiers, evidently waiting to be loaded on boats" (XII, p. 66).

This picture does not make the author happy. Commerce has destroyed the beauty of the village meadow and transformed the haystacks into a monotonous row of numbers, which still stand on the riverbank, but then they will move to the "Herald of Finance," to stock market accounts, to summaries of the Ministry of Finance, and to the Berlin and London trade telegrams.

Just as monotonous are the sawmills on the banks of the Sheksna, the wooden barges, and the tugboats. Even the Sheksna itself, according to Uspensky

seems to think only about the state budget and, constantly shifting and meandering, worries only about how to create better docks. Now it makes a huge semi-circle, apparently without any purpose. But if you realized that nothing took place here without the participation of that thread, one end of which is hidden there at the apex of the budget, you would immediately understand: The Sheksna encircles a large area and because of this, gives an opportunity to unload in different places from the same meadow instead of having to take the loads to one place. It does this, clearly, in order to support government aims.

It did this, continues the writer, so that

when a cargo is loaded quickly, our country can announce quicker than other countries that "the position of oats, hay, and wheat is strong," and thereby, get a chance "to answer with disdain the threatening articles of the North German General Newspaper" inspired, of course, by the Iron Chancellor himself, that is, Bismarck. (XII, 67)

Uspensky paid particular attention to the man working with machines in factories. The question of the "power of the machine" was, in Uspensky's view, a part of the question of the "power of capital." In his letter of July 14, 1889 to V. Lavrov—one of the editors of the journal, *Russkaya mysl*—Uspensky told about his plan to write a series of sketches under the general title of "The Power of the Machine" in which he would show the influence of machine on man (XIV, p. 315). Uspensky did not carry out his plan; he did not write "The Power of Capital" or "The Power of the Machine." But among his papers is a fragment of an essay entitled "Machine and Man" (1889), which has been published (XII, p. 483). In it Uspensky acknowledged the advent of the machine in Russian life. Uspensky's works contain comments on the positive role of the machine and all kinds of technical improvement, which shows that in his search for an ideal life Uspensky did not confine himself to thinking in terms of peasant life with his primitive tools.

Uspensky saw that under the conditions of his time the machine killed the man in the worker ("Miroshnik"). In the story "The Career of Petka" ("Pet'kina kar'era") (1886), Uspensky told about the sad transformation of Petka, a peasant lad, into a "machinelike person." Petka's "competition" with capital and machine could end only with death. This tragic story showed that Uspensky had taken a good look at the new generation of people who grew up near the machine and worked with it. Uspensky tried to understand their psychology which was so different from that of the peasant. What most interested and pleased Uspensky about Petka was "not his cap and flaming red shirt, but an upsurge of spirit and moral regeneration which I just could not explain" (X_1, p. 82). In the story, Uspensky considered the conditions of factory work and concluded that the "upsurge of spirit" in Petka was due to the fact that Petka now earned wages, that he changed from a useless inhabitant in the village, from a downtrodden and dejected person, into someone who was independent.

There was no doubt that the urban proletariat often looked back to the village and dreamed of returning to the soil. In his sketch "Journey from Kama to Perm," Uspensky discussed the Russian miner's song ("That the miner's life is cursed . . ."); he understood the unspoken hopes of the tormented miner who was formerly a peasant. "His ideal," said Uspensky,

is the village, his work with the soil. . . . His ideals are found in his charming dreams about old times, in the strange, incomprehensible wisdom of nature whose commands one obeys without grumble and criticism, and therefore it is so easy for one to feel good in the soul, having nothing to answer for in one's life.

Uspensky, however, did not commend the miner's daydreaming about the village. Though the life of a miner was also a life of strenuous toil, Uspensky took a cynical attitude toward an ideal of happiness based on old times. He could not regard these "charming dreams" of the worker with joy, for they led to a withdrawal from culture, from one's will and mind, from the conscious participation in the "great chain of victories of the human genius" (XI, p. 536).

The cheerless picture of life of the Russian miner is found in the notes, *New Folk Songs* (*Novye narodnye stishki*) (1889). The fate of the Russian miner, said Uspensky, consisted in "backbreaking work," "relaxation" in the public house, and then "exhaustion and disappearance from the face of the earth." The miner "cannot even conceive of any other course of life" (XII, p. 57).[6]

In this respect, continued Uspensky, the workers in Western Europe had gone farther. They did not tie their hopes to the past or to instinctive submission to the "strange wisdom" of nature, but rather placed them in the "future, in the achievements of the mind, in that which man has thought and made, which testifies to human wisdom." Whereas the Russian worker had only recently been torn away from the land and the manor house and had not yet gotten accustomed to the new ideals of life, Western European workers closely identified themselves with these ideals, were able to take pride in the victories achieved by man, and lived in an atmosphere of conscious struggle, in the belief that to participate in the "victory of human genius" was "happiness and honor" (XI, p. 536).

Uspensky did not mean to idealize the conditions of life of the Western European proletariat. He clearly saw that the worker in the West was transformed by capital into a wheel of a big chariot of great victories for the present and future. But to Uspensky the important fact was that the proletariat in the West looked to the future, desired learning and refinement, regarded itself as participant in history, entered into struggle, and was confident of its own strength. The Russian worker of that time was still not sufficiently aware of his position, though he was beginning to awaken. Uspensky was happy to see that capitalism had not yet succeeded in purchasing the soul of the worker and he noted all the little signs which showed that the "more experienced worker is beginning, from time to time, to feel wrath, shame, and . . . will get angry."

III *"Meeting" with Marx*

In studying the fate of Russia, the people of Western Europe, and the struggle of the working masses, Uspensky turned to Marxism. Marx—whose *Das Kapital* was first published in Russian in St. Petersburg in 1872 and was given a great deal of publicity in the Russian press—was well known to Uspensky in the 1870's. At that time, however, Marx's ideas had no influence on Uspensky's thinking with respect to the development of mankind. In the second half of the 1880's Uspensky tried to determine whether or not Marx's opinions about the fate of Russia and Western Europe were correct. What Uspensky wanted to know was: which explanation of Russia's economic life was the correct one, that of Marx or that of the Populists?

This question was the subject of a short cycle of essays under the general title of *Terrible Sins* (1888). It was published in *Russkaya mysl* at the time when Uspensky was working on his article "Bitter Reproach," written as a result of the publication of Marx's famous letter to the magazine *Otechestvennye zapiski*.

A comparison of the third essay in this cycle, entitled "Details about the Unexpected Confusion. The Advent of Mr. Dividend. Traces of a Dark Past" ("Gospodin Kupon") [referred to subsequently as "The Advent of Mr. Dividend"] with "Bitter Reproach" shows that the two works are closely related. "There are views," he said in "The Advent of Mr. Dividend,"

that place [the bourgeois system] . . . in a completely different light; there are intelligent people who have first-hand knowledge of this system, that is, who have studied it at the place of its origin, in Europe, who look at this question completely differently. The leveling of the whole society, that is, of all kinds of "instruments" [i.e., the people] from the enormous to the smallest will, as it were, equalize all members of maimed mankind in an attempt to find a way out from the trap; moreover, our profuse talks about the peasant and about how he "does everything by himself," and so on, are considered propaganda that completely departs from the general opinion. . . . A bear den! That's what "the labor of one's own hands" is, my dear brother! . . . Yes, brother, there do exist such views on hard-working farmers! What can you do? Indeed, for some insensible person there is no better place than the village [to hide in, like] a bear den; he can live there for ages and not be emotionally disturbed in any way. But this is not right, since all around us are poverty, sorrow, and sin. We must think hard about this matter. Perhaps, and it may be true, that the evil doings of contemporary capitalism will eventually lead to general, universal striving toward the building of a life that would be for the good of all, I do not know! (XI, pp. 373-74)

This passage reveals Uspensky's different emotions as he examined the question of capitalism: the fear for the fate of the "fully intellectual person" who might be transformed into an "instrument"; a bitter and ironical attitude towards his own "profuse talks" about a life based on "labor of one's own hands" with the soil; and the striving to look ahead without fear, to understand the teaching of the "intelligent people" about the ways of saving man, and about the good and evil sides of capitalism. Uspensky had to admit that the village which he loved was only a "bear den," a "corner of Buddhist-like tranquility" for insensible people who took no notice of the sufferings around them.

In "The Advent of Mr. Dividend" Uspensky was perplexed by questions of "something will happen" and "how to understand it." The essay is marked by a sad, lyrical tone. The article "Bitter Reproach," on the other hand, had been written in a completely different key. In Marx's letter to *Otechestvennye zapiski* Uspensky found the answers to the questions that had deeply tormented him and were the cause of his constant anxiety.

At this point, it is necessary to say a few words about the publication of Marx's letter in *Otechestvennye zapiski*. The letter was a reply to an article by Nikolay Mikhaylovsky that had appeared in the same journal (October, 1877) in the "Contemporary Review" section. The article is entitled "Karl Marx Before the Court of Mr. Zhukovsky." *Otechestvennye zapiski*, edited by Saltyov-Shchedrin, Mikhaylovsky, and Nekrasov (who died in December, 1877) had come out in support of Marx's economic theories. In 1872, when the Russian translation of *Das Kapital* appeared, the journal—with which Uspensky was closely associated at the time—published an article by Mikhaylovsky entitled "On the Occasion of the Publication of Marx's Book in Russia." Mikhaylovsky, a Populist, could not understand or accept Marx's concept of socialism and the revolutionary proletariat, but, nevertheless, in his article he spoke sympathetically about the author of *Das Kapital.* Against the background of the time, this in itself was something significant. It will be recalled that the liberal journal, *Vestnik Evropy,* had in 1877 published an article by a former editor of *Sovremennik,* Yu. Zhukovsky, the economist, entitled "K. Marx and his Book on Capital"; another former editor of *Sovremennik,* Maxim A. Antonovich, wrote a pamphlet called "The Theory of Value." In their works both writers abandoned their former progressive positions and launched a violent attack against Marx, distorting Marx's theories, and denying their originality.

This led *Otechestvennye zapiski* to come out in defense of Marx; the act shows the integrity of the editors of the journal as progressive liberals. The defense was in the form of the above-mentioned article by Mikhaylovsky, who pointed out the bankruptcy of bourgeois economics in its fight against Marx's economic theories. However, at the same time, he gave an incorrect and oversimplified interpretation of Marx's views on the development of mankind. According to Mikhaylovsky, Marx was fatalistic in his outlook and considered that all nations must inevitably, repeating each other, pass the capitalist stage in their economic development.

This interpretation aroused strong reaction from Marx who considered it necessary to send a reply to *Otechestvennye zapiski* and explain his views on the historical destiny of man.

The letter was written in November, 1877, but not sent. Marx was afraid that its publication in *Otechestvennye zapiski* would endanger the existence of the journal. The letter was written in French and apparently had not been corrected by Marx. After his death it was found among his papers by Engels, who made copies of it and sent one of them together with his comments to Vera Zasulich in Geneva in 1884. She probably made the first Russian translation of the letter. It appeared in Russia clandestinely in mimeographed form. However, prior to this, Marx's letter had been circulated in Russia for some time in handwritten French copies. Like everything else written by

Marx, the letter received widespread attention in Russian intellectual circles and was given various interpretations.

The letter was published for the first time in Geneva in 1886
in the journal, *Vestnik Narodnoy voli* (No. 5). In Russia, it
appeared in print for the first time in *Yuridichesky vestnik* in
October, 1888, and it was this publication that attracted Uspensky's attention.

Saltykov-Shchedrin and others associated with *Otechestvennye
zapiski* undoubtedly knew of this letter by Marx. But Saltykov-
Shchedrin made no comment on the letter, as he was generally
silent on Marx's writings.

Mikhaylovsky thought that Marx had at first failed to consider the historical peculiarities of Russia and thus predicted
that Russia would go through all the difficulties of the capitalist
phase. Mikhaylovsky further believed that it was only after
Marx had read his remarkable article "Karl Marx Before the
Court of Mr. Zhukovsky" that Marx had changed his point of
view and rejected fatalism. Mikhaylovsky, said Plekhanov,
was proud of the letter by Marx because it proved that he—
Mikhaylovsky—was right. Commenting on the incident, Plekhanov quoted the words of Lermontov: "All this would have been
funny if it were not so sad."

Of all the literary figures, writers on social problems, and
members of the revolutionary liberation movement in Russia at
the end of the last century, Uspensky was the only one who
paid special attention to Marx's letter. Uspensky pointed out
its scientific, social, and moral significance, and felt that he
should write an article on it. He thus helped to publicize the
words of Marx. But most important was Uspensky's interpretation of the letter, an interpretation which revealed Uspensky's
keen insight and brilliant arguments. Uspensky, as will be seen
later, pointed out that Marx's views on the future of Russia
and Western Europe had not changed, that they did not need
corrections from Russian thinkers, notably from Mikhaylovsky,
and that Marx was never a fatalist in his outlook.

Marx's letter affected Uspensky deeply. He expressed regret
that the Russian press had practically paid no attention to the
letter and suggested to V. Sobolevsky, editor of *Russkie vedomosti*, among others, that he publish excerpts from it in his
newspaper. Finally, in the latter part of December, 1888 Uspen-

sky sent to the *Volzhsky vestnik*—a newspaper published in the city of Kazan—an article entitled "Bitter Reproach." Not meeting censorship requirements, it was not published there. Alexander I. Ertel tried to publish it in an anthology which he planned to put out for the benefit of the Voronezh public library, but Uspensky refused to send him the article.[7]

The manuscript of "Bitter Reproach" however, became well known among intellectuals in Kazan, who respected Uspensky greatly. Uspensky had visited Kazan a number of times and was there in August, 1888 (XIV, p. 223). V. N. Polyak, chief editor of *Volzhsky vestnik*, in an unpublished letter to Uspensky told him that "Bitter Reproach" had failed to be approved by the censor, but that it was passing from hand to hand there. "I am requested to ask your permission to have several copies made of it, since there are very many who want to read it."[8] It is worth noting that one of the copies of Uspensky's article was found in the possession of Nikolay E. Fedoseev, a member of the Marxist circle in Kazan, at the time of his arrest.[9]

Parts of "Bitter Reproach" first became known to the public in 1902 in Polyak's reminiscences about Uspensky.[10] Only in 1933 was it published in full by Nikolay K. Piksanov in *Novy mir* (No. 3). The manuscript was in the possession of Polyak who gave it to the manuscript department of the Pushkin House.

"Bitter Reproach" is a morally and intellectually stimulating article. It is concise and serious; in it Uspensky tried to answer questions that had long tormented him. Marx's letter helped him to understand many things. As Uspensky said to V. Sobolevsky: "How touched I was by this letter! This is Marx. Not Leo Tolstoy,[11] not Vyshnegradsky,[12] not Kotkov"[13] (XIV, p. 198). "No!" emphasized Uspensky in "Bitter Reproach,"

this is not a patriot from Moscow calling for the encouragement of "production" by means of financial remuneration; this is not a "populist" with his sincere love of the beautiful, carefully gathering flowers that bring joy to the soul . . . ; this is not a "Marxist" who says that the flowers gathered by the populist must nonetheless die in view of the fatalistic theories of capitalism. (XII, p. 113)

In his study of economics, Marx used an approach based on entirely new and genuinely scientific principles. What Uspensky particularly appreciated was that Marx as a scholar did not separate "the phenomena of our life into those that are pleasant and those that are not," but regarded them as a whole and extracted from them "the real, unblemished truth" (XII, p. 10).

In "Bitter Reproach" Uspensky said that "he particularly valued the impartial word of such a man as Marx...." Uspensky noted the scholarly integrity of Marx whose study of Russian life was thorough and detailed. Uspensky was amazed to find that the author of *Das Kapital* took the trouble to learn the Russian language in order to be able really to understand Russian life.

Uspensky fully agreed with Marx's view on the economic situation in Russia. The conclusion reached by Marx in the letter of 1877 to *Otechestvennye zapiski* was that "if Russia continues to pursue the path she has followed since 1861, she will lose the finest chance ever offered by history to a people and undergo all the fatal vicissitudes of the capitalist regime." Elsewhere in the letter Marx said:

If Russia is tending to become a capitalist nation after the example of the West-European countries—and during the last few years she has been taking a lot of trouble in this direction—she will not succeed without having first transformed a good part of her peasants into proletarians and after that, once taken to the bosom of the capitalist régime, she will experience its pitiless laws like other profane peoples.[14]

While noting that Russia had for some years been developing into a capitalist nation, Marx avoided "giving a definite answer," and refrained "from making an analysis of the facts of Russian life,"[15] that is, on the question of how Russia would develop further. Marx used the conditional form: "If Russia...," etc.

The question arises as to why Marx in 1877 refrained from giving a definite opinion about the economic development of Russia. There were important reasons for this. By not giving a definite answer on the question, Marx showed that his views on the history of mankind were not at all fatalistic or dogmatic as assumed by Mikhaylovsky. Russian liberal Populists interpreted Marx's "logic" as follows: inasmuch as Western Europe was on the capitalist path Russia must, with fatal inevitability, take this path as well. Then there were Russian bourgeois economists who, in one way or another, used *Das Kapital* for their own purposes and presented a vulgar "logic" as the essence of the economic theories of Marx. What Marx did in his letter was to point out these errors and distortions.

"Bitter Reproach" can—in a way—be taken to mean that Uspensky in 1888, eleven years after Marx wrote his letter for *Otechestvennye zapiski*, still hoped "to mend matters," that is, he still hoped that Russia could avoid capitalist development; and that after coming to know Marx's "bitter reproach" sent "to us from beyond the grave" he considered it advisable to start carrying out those social obligations that would save Russia from the "bitter cup" of capitalist development. Marx's letter, in Uspensky's words, was a "terrible and bitter reproach against Russian society for committing that great sin against itself,"— for allowing the development of capitalism in Russia.

In these words one can hear echoes of Populist illusions which remained with Uspensky to the end. However, generally speaking, it would be wrong to interpret Uspensky's article as a Populist document. This is shown by Uspensky's letter to V. M. Sobolevsky dated November 3, 1888, in which Uspensky said that Marx's "bitter reproach" was correct and that his letter to *Otechestvennye zapiski* was a "death sentence" for those who continued to hope that the Russian village community setup (*obshchina*) would save Russia from the West European evil.

Marx also passed a "death sentence" on Uspensky's ideals. But regret did not prevent Uspensky from facing the truth. Marx's letter did not make Uspensky think that Russia still had a chance to escape capitalist development; on the contrary it convinced him that such a possibility did not exist in the conditions of the 1880's. It is noteworthy that in "Bitter Reproach" Uspensky did not have one word to say about the village community setup (*obshchina*) as a unique Russian phenomenon.

The collapse of the movement "to go to the people," the breakup of *Narodnaya volya*, the social apathy of the intelligentsia, and the economic development of the country since 1877, the year Marx wrote his letter, convinced Uspensky that Russia had missed her "wonderful opportunity," and that she would continue along the capitalist path on which she had embarked, as Marx had pointed out, in 1861.

This does not mean, however, that in "Bitter Reproach" Uspensky had become a Marxist. There is no question that Uspensky was influenced by Marx's ideas which had helped him to understand the economic and social reality of his time. But nevertheless, in "Bitter Reproach" Uspensky remained a peasant democrat of prerevolutionary Russia. Besides sensitive and wise thoughts occasioned by Marx's letter, there is in "Bitter Reproach" another tendency: Uspensky turned his social thoughts into personal, moral reflections. The title "Bitter Reproach" indicates this, as well as its semi-imaginative and semi-journalistic style. Uspensky found in Marx's letter "reproachful words for all of us," "the genuine, the brightest and bitterest truth about the state of our life...." Marx, said Uspensky, expressed in his letter "regret and sorrow"; Marx "expresses sorrow over the fact that man must become the victim of these mistakes [in economic development.]"

The style of "Bitter Reproach" shows that Uspensky had translated Marx's teaching into an emotional-psychological language and adapted the teaching to his own moral scheme. This represents a certain narrow-mindedness, but it is understandable against the background of the time. On the whole, "Bitter Reproach" is one of the most outstanding works by a Russian liberal publicist of the epoch in which Marxist ideas had just began to be known in Russia and had begun to conquer the minds of the proletariat and democratic intellectuals.

IV The Art of Uspensky in the 1880's

Some of Uspensky's contemporaries felt that in his last years Uspensky had ceased to be an artist and had turned entirely to journalistic and sociological subjects. This is not so. In this last period Uspensky continued to produce works that were imaginative and full of humor, as all his creative works are. His humor varies in content and form; and this is related to the evolution of his attitudes towards reality. Referring to the early years of his creative life, Uspensky said that though his soul suffered hellish agonies, he laughed. And, indeed, in *The Manners of Rasteryaeva Street* and other works of the 1860's, Uspensky used humor as a defense against the acute anxiety he felt over the fate of the "people picked to the bone." In these works, one does not yet sense the pain which fills his writings of the 1870's and especially, of the 1880's. Nevertheless, humor remained Uspensky's faithful weapon even in the last years of his life.

Let us take, for example, one of Uspensky's best stories, "Incubator Chick" ("Parovoy Tsyplyonok") (1888) which made a great impression on Leo Tolstoy. The story recreates a conversation between peasants about the soil. The main narrator, a specialist in "chicken psychology," that is, a poultry breeder, maintains that a chick grown from an incubator has no soul; it walks and eats its food but has "no ability to think." Listening to this, someone says that the Bible talks about the Christian soul but says nothing about a chicken's soul. The conversation then drifts into talk of a more general character. Someone mentions the recent death of a local tavern keeper. The question is: how did he manage to break his back under the railroad car, but not his arm or leg. The specialist on chicken psychology answers that the reason the tavern keeper died was because his soul and conscience were ailing.

Next, Seliverstov, the poultry breeder, assures everyone that there *is* such a thing as a "chicken soul" and with a fair amount of humor explains the difference between a chicken raised in a "steam chick plant,"—that is, an incubator—and a chicken raised by an ordinary setting hen which gives its descendants the "qualities of a soul":

A chicken, my boy, doesn't like to sit on eggs very much.... She wants only to lay an egg, and then go out to café-restaurants with the roosters, sing a few songs, and cackle to herself.... There are such dandies among them that you can keep one sitting on eggs in a basket for three days, and she huddles to the side of the basket and doesn't sit on them, thinking, as any other lady would: "If I have children myself, then maybe I'll ruin my bust and no one will love me!"... And she huddles in the corner, and the eggs lie there without any attention at all.... Take off the basket cover on the fourth day and—swoosh!—she runs away, cackles, yells, complains to the whole chicken-yard about being cooped up. And the rooster, acting like crazy is already running to her defense: he is also compassionate! He takes her into the bushes... to a masquerade. Sometimes such a swaggering hen comes out [of the basket] that she is unmanageable! Here's what the old women do with swaggerers like that: they'll take and make some bread balls, soak them in vodka, and give them to the hens to eat.... The swaggering hen will eat them and get drunk. Then they put the drunken hen on eggs and close the basket.... While she's sleeping and doesn't think of masquerade balls, the first thing you know she gets to know the eggs.... The heat goes to the egg and from the egg to her.... Take off the cover—and she can't get up! And she knows herself how nice it would be to go out; she hears the rooster crow, sing his love songs... and she still can't get up—her conscience has touched her! She now has pity! Her soul has begun to speak.... And she'll keep sitting until her belly is nothing but raw meat. Not a single feather will be left on it. She'll sit until it hurts. And what for? Because of conscience!... And because of this conscience, she'll start thinking about different things: How she was when she was a pullet (after all, she has to sit for a long time and there's a lot to think about under the bench), and how she used to go out, and what she saw, and which rooster jumped up to her, and what kind of feathers he had (she would remember each feather; think about it a hundred times), and how it was later—how she got sick, how she got heavy, how she gave birth, and how she squawked when she gave birth.... She would think of all this while she is under the bench.... And all of these thoughts of hers pass from her soul to the chick's soul, and the chick inherits all of her ideas and worries.... He still hardly looks like anything, but the setting hen has already given him all the things needed by the soul; all ideas ... they're like little seeds, as if made by a pinprick: here and there, and later, they grow up to be real big chicken ideas.... This, my boys, isn't a fifty-degree temperature or whatever it is, but a soul speaking with a soul! ... So the hen thought and sighed, how she was a young chicken and how everything then turned out—and all this goes into the soul of the cold-hearted chick.... How come so many roosters are born? Because the hen dreams about the rooster more than anything else. She remembers every feather.... And does the temperature [i.e. the incubator] think at all about a chicken's life? Does it think about roosters? About how boring it is to sit under a bench, but there's nothing else to do because you feel sorry for the child? It doesn't think at all! And what do you get?—A chick without a soul, without conscience, without worries, and without a brain! ... And grass won't grow either from an 'lectric light.... The soul—that's one thing, and inventions—another.... No, this isn't nonsense.... You have to think it over very carefully! (X$_2$, 294-95)

This discussion about the soul is considered nonsense by the young assistant to the railroad stationmaster who happens to be passing by. The young man has just recently been hired and gotten married; he has on a new uniform and feels like someone who belongs to refined society. He is on his way home to his wife and his steaming samovar, and his whole bearing indicates that he is satisfied with things and that nothing can worry him. He is totally absorbed in his own thoughts which are far away from the subject of the conversation between the peasants. Meanwhile, the conversation turns into general gossiping and ends with the bitter words of one of the peasants who had been silent up to then, a peasant who is in debt: "... we peasants are getting worse and worse off all the time from all these inventions ... they squeeze us from all sides ... and there're the taxes we've got to pay...."

These words of an ordinary peasant and Uspensky's comments on them give an ironic twist to the humor of the story. "The 'grey' peasant," Uspensky said, "made all the peasants turn their thoughts back to reality, and thus ended a casual conversation in a way in which all our conversations end nowadays, no matter what the subject they started with (X_2, p. 296).

This turn from humor to sad irony gives the story a general meaning. It reveals the essence of a phenomenon, namely, that the working people only became worse off with all kinds of inventions. Of significance here is the contrast between someone belonging to "refined society" who was concerned with his personal life only and the ordinary people seeking answers to urgent questions of life.

In Uspensky's works, topical questions, journalistic exposure, and critical analysis were combined with artistic form, imaginative approach, and humor. This is shown in another interesting story: "Coachman with a Device" ("Izvozchik s apparatom") (1889) from the cycle of sketches entitled *No Way of Joining the Ends*. The story is a humorous recreation of a discussion among ordinary people about various kinds of inventions, in particular, about the conveniences and inconveniences of using the services of a coachman whose carriage is equipped with a counting device. But the story is not merely humorous, for the discussion soon centers on a serious question.

The people of simple calling began to consider the question about the counting device from a standpoint that was most important for them: "will it benefit us?" It turned out that they got nothing from this new invention. Even the coachman got nothing but evil from it. (XI, p. 331)

Quite different were the views of "refined society," as expressed in newspaper columns. Members of this society were pleased with the device which would control the coachman and make him utterly insignificant. The newspaper columnists had nothing to say about the fate of the victim. This attitude of the author toward "refined society" expressed in the second part of the story gives the story a new tone and throws light on the meaning of the entire sketch cycle. The story, which begins with humor, ends not in sad irony as in the case of "Incubator Chick," but in expressions of spiritual torment on the part of the author who was distressed by the fact that the common people received no benefit from the new device and by the indifference of "refined society" to the fate of the coachman who was brought to a "dead silence" by a hopeless life. The views of "refined society" and Uspensky's comments on them form the most interesting and significant parts of the entire cycle and illustrate a characteristic feature of Uspensky's works: in a cycle of journalistic sketches the main thought is expressed in imaginative form.

This cycle opens with the story "He Got Angry!" It is a humorous one about tricks used by students who cheated on their examinations. The comic situation, however, provided Uspensky with an opportunity to consider Russian life in general. On the one hand there were the secondary school students—the future intelligentsia and "refined society"—who began to learn how to cheat early in life. On the other hand, there were the people—the exhausted migrant workers—who expected the intelligentsia to improve their lot. Uspensky asked:

Is it possible that both the students and the working people are members of the same society? Is it possible that these students will become the future leaders and pillars of society? And how can the people count on help from those who began their life by cheating?

Thus, Uspensky defined the main problems of the cycle: namely, that the two extremes of Russian life—the people and the students (the future intelligentsia)—did not meet. "It is impossible," said Uspensky, "to convey those torments which overcame me when I thought about the differences between these two extremes, both of which belong to the same society" (XI, p. 243).

In this story a comic scene (in which a merchant-father gets

angry with his son who takes part in stealing examination papers)
is combined with reflections about a "chaotic society" in which
the extremes—the poor working people and the intelligentsia—
could not be joined.

This theme appears again and is summed up in the last story
of the cycle: "Coachman with a Device." The seemingly innocent tricks of a student are linked to the invention of a device
for controlling the coachman and making the life of "refined
society"—the former students—easier. The gap between the
"dirty people" and "refined society" pained Uspensky, who
recalled the preceding generation of idealistic intellectuals who
were able to serve the people. But the intelligentsia had changed;
its world had become a "happy swampland." Saddened by society's indifference to the life of the people, Uspensky ends his
story about the coachman with question: "What will happen
next?" (XI, p. 338).

In these two stories the "evil of the day" is treated with humor
and given a general sociological and even philosophical meaning. Uspensky commented on the life of the Russian people as
a whole: a life characterized by hopelessness on the part of
the common people and the inability of the intelligentsia to
serve the people. But Uspensky sometimes used still another
approach—the lyrical approch. He emphasized the psychological
aspect of a social question and considered it in terms of the
fate of an individual. This is shown in his sketch "Something
Went to His Head" ("Vbrelo v bashku") (1888), about a village
inhabitant, from the cycle, *Koy pro chto* (*A Little About Something*).

The hero of the story is a peasant named Ivan Alifanov, whose
every action, thought, and feeling is tied to the back-breaking
work which he does everyday. One year, there is an unusually
rich harvest which blesses the area with warmth and tranquility,
with sweet and good rest. The harvest also has a tremendous
psychological effect on Ivan Alifanov. Uspensky shows how,
under the influence of the unexpected state of well-being, Ivan
Alifanov—both his body and soul—become "thawed." His head
becomes clearer; he begins to have a wish to read a book or
listen to someone reading, to figure out what life is about, to
think about himself. In a lyrical style Uspensky describes how
his hero gradually becomes adjusted to his new situation—that

of a man who has time to rest. First Ivan Alifanov speaks about
the "rights of his body trampled upon by life," and then about
his soul.

With pain he relived his entire past life which he had all but forgotten because he had never had time to think about it. His life of
back-breaking toil now seemed intolerable to him. And then suddenly,
unexpectedly ... in his heart full of pain and in his lonesome mind
... appeared the image of Annushka, a girl whom Ivan Alifanov
had loved as a lad.

But, the parents had opposed the marriage, and as a result, his
life had become "forty-five years of endless hard toil," "under
the most horrible conditions" (X_1, p. 221). His love for Annushka
was the only beautiful thing, "the only real joy" in his life. Then
his thoughts went to the "base relations" between him and Anisya,
his wife, whom he did not love and whom he found inhuman.
Compared with Annushka, his wife seemed a rough and wild
woman. Ivan Alifanov began to feel torments of conscience,
bitterness, and shame. He was overcome with fear and appeared
to be on the verge of moral and physical collapse....

In this lyrical story, "Something Went to His Head," the
liberation from the "power of the soil" led to a catastrophe. But
the story of Ivan Alifanov has a different meaning from that of
Ivan Bosykh, the hero of The Power of the Soil. Bosykh, after
being freed from back-breaking work with the soil, became
corrupted and ceased to be a human being. The opposite happened with Ivan Alifanov: Liberation from farm labor meant
the beginning of an understanding of the senselessness and
abnormality of his life. It is this understanding that is the theme
of the story, and the personal story of Ivan Alifanov was meant
to be taken as a typical example of village life.

Here we have not only a writer who was able to create a vivid
and moving story of one peasant and describe an isolated "living
fact" that attracted his attention, but also a thinker who analyzed
his material and penetrated into the very heart of a way of life.
To take an ordinary, everyday incident and reveal its social
meaning, to show its dependence on the general and basic conditions of life—herein lies the power of real art. The secret of
such art was possessed by Uspensky.

In his long semi-imaginative and semi-journalistic cycles

Uspensky usually included stories and imaginative sketches which are of great importance for understanding the cycles as a whole. An example of this is the story, "Coachman with a Device." Even in those cycles such as *Letter from a Journey* and *Visits to Migrants,* which are purely journalistic and contain no independent stories, Uspensky used images, imaginative scenes, dialogues, and short sketches. One needs to look carefully into the texture of Uspensky's journalistic writings to realize that they are highly imaginative. In them the lyrical is combined with the analytical, the personal with the objective portrayal of life, the comic with the tragic, humor with satire.

For example, in the *Visits to the Migrants* (*Poezdki k pereselentsam*), Uspensky tells of peasants whose dreams of having the right to own land take them ... to far-off Siberia, where they hope to get the sweet taste of that right. But these childish dreams of the migrant peasants are soon shattered into bits by reality. A family is given five rubles and told that "there cannot even be any further talk of any other kind of help." A crowd gathers to discuss the matter ...

"What's going on here?" babbles a migrant through pale lips—weak from hunger and weariness, and most of all from fear for the future—holding a five-ruble note in his shaking hand.

He stands as if in a stupor.

"It's all very simple. You want to wipe us poor people off the face of the earth! ... There will be more room. ... Now, this all seems very simple to us!"

This idea has only to be thrown out into the crowd of migrants surrounding the poor fellow standing thunderstruck with his five rubles and it immediately gets full support from the crowd.

"That's right! That's right!" is heard from the crowd. "If they didn't want to completely ruin us poor peasants, they'd lure the rich and not the poor to migrate! The rich should be moved! A rich man has money and everything! He can get along in a new place with no problems. And they lure us just to play a dirty trick on us. ... Just so they can lead us away from our places, and once they do—to let us die. They couldn't care less!"

"Yeah! It's nothing but pure fraud! ... If it weren't a filthy trick, they'd have to escort us at every stage [that is, give them free food. N.P.]. That's what they'd have to do if they would treat us honestly! ... Horse thieves and crooks are escorted that way. ... Why do we have to beg? ..." (XI, p. 71-72)

Uspensky's multi-voiced dialogues fulfill characterizing functions. In short, volatile remarks, his peasant heroes show expressive lexical-intonation qualities, which permit the reader to visualize the speaker, his social and moral outlook, and the unique quality of his speech.

Mass dialogues included by Uspensky give the tense feelings of a crowd. There is also extended discussion and arguments about questions of life, which draw in more and more participants, and short, but strong and vicious remarks thrown out against the authorities.

"Which province are you fellows from?" asks a gendarme who has nothing to do, turning to a crowd of scythemen, who are hungry and ragged, and are waiting for something on the platform.

"Go to hell with your province!" someone answers him from the crowd.

And the gendarme was experienced enough not to "hear" this insolent answer. (IX, p. 396)

These mass dialogues, revealing the thoughts and feelings of the people, are written with great skill and in them, Uspensky succeeded in reproducing true folk speech.

V   Discouraging Results and Uspensky's Spiritual Tragedy

In his fairy tale Adventures with Kramolnikov (1886), Saltykov-Shchedrin portrayed a Russian writer who resembled Uspensky. "Kramolnikov," wrote Saltykov-Shchedrin,

was passionately devoted to his country and had an excellent knowledge of her past and present. But this knowledge had a peculiar effect on him; it was a constant source of pain which finally dominated him. The pain gave him a direction and colored all his activity, and he not only made no attempt to get rid of the pain, but nursed it and kept it alive in his heart. To feel the pain enabled him to create characters through whom the pain was transmitted to others.[16]

Characterizing Kramolnikov, Saltykov-Shchedrin pointed out that the purpose of Kramolnikov's work was to keep alive in the hearts of his contemporaries the belief that a bright future lay ahead. Uspensky also had similar beliefs, which gave him relief from his constant pain. But he also saw that reality had destroyed his hopes—those happy moments during which he could forget the problems of life. While the intelligentsia was preoccupied with questions of "how to live a holy life" and "what to do," Uspensky was asking how the common people really lived (IX, pp. 271, 280). Many times Uspensky realized that the truth was not where he, his friends, the writers of his time, or the intellectual Populists, had hoped to find it.

The pain experienced by Uspensky, brought about by the conditions of life, became extremely acute. Uspensky not only explained "where rags and hunger came from," but, to use the words of Saltykov-Shchedrin, felt "that deep pain which forces him to identify himself with the needs of society and to bear on his own shoulders the sins of the world." Uspensky experienced similar pain earlier; however, in the last period of his life he became a writer for whom the sufferings of the common people were his own sufferings. "He writes not merely from his heart, but from a bleeding heart," noted a number of critics of the time in discussing Uspensky's new attitude toward the life of the people.[17]

This new attitude can best be seen in the unfinished cycles of sketches about "living numbers," about people who were merely small fractions of the whole: "A Quarter of a Horse" ("'Chetvert' loshadi") (1887), "Receipt" ("Kvitantsiya"), ("Supplement to the Story 'Receipt'" ("Dopolnenie k rasskazu 'Kvitantsiya'"), "Zero!" ("Nol'tselykh!") (1888). In the sketches of this unfinished cycle, Uspensky turned cold official statistics about semi-feudal Russia undergoing capitalist development into imaginative characters that tell us about everyday human sufferings. In these sketches he unites great truthfulness in analyzing the life of people reduced to fractions of a whole—to numbers—by social and economic conditions with great art in which numbers from statistical tables are turned into living characters. Added to these elements is the suffering experienced by Uspensky as he observed the life of poor people and tried to protect them from injustice. V. G. Korolenko characterized the story "Receipt" as a "heartbreaking cry of a pure soul."[18]

Uspensky knew only too well what it meant to have to pay taxes without having land and what was "pain compressed into a small number"—the sufferings of a peasant family that owned only a quarter of a horse. This was also Uspensky's pain. He believed that numbers told the "real truth," and to be a fraction

of a whole and not to have even the slightest notion about the
right to life was the fate of the common people. For Uspensky
numbers represented the tragic fate of the people. He studied
the "zeroes" and was "moved to tears" ("Receipt"). "Three
Terrible Zeroes" was the title of one of his sketches; the three
zeroes being found in the budget of a village: for schools—0,
for hospitals—0, for social welfare—0.

Uspensky was shocked by what he found out about the life
of the people and concluded that the situation of the peasant
was a hopeless one. The type of ordinary working man who,
in Uspensky's conception, was both owner and worker was
disappearing from Russia. The working peasantry, which was
particularly dear to Uspensky's heart and with which his ideals
were linked, faced a bleak future. This was one of the causes
of Uspensky's spiritual torment. He was unhappy with the
results of the revolutionary struggle of the intelligentsia. Beginning with the period 1859-1861, he had several times seen the
shattering of revolutionary hopes and the loss of the best people
of Russia. In the decade following 1861, Russian revolutionaries,
while heroically trying to inspire the people to struggle, remained
isolated and were becoming ever fewer in number due to tsarist
repression. "I constantly find myself in a desert and alone;
there is no one to say a word to," wrote Uspensky when some
of his close friends were arrested (XIII, p. 394). As he watched
the failure of the revolutionaries and saw his own hopes and
ideals being destroyed, Uspensky became convinced that the
forces leading the struggle for the liberation of the people were
too weak. E. Letkova once heard Uspensky say despondently:
"And the soul of the people becomes emptier and emptier. How
should one fight against this? Is there such a force? I don't
see it at present, I don't see it...."[19]

Uspensky felt oppressed by "loathsome reality": the political
reaction of the 1880's, the betrayal by the intelligentsia of the
ideological legacy of the 1860's and 1870's, and the prevalence
of the petty bourgeois point of view in the press, in art, and
in social behavior. In a number of his works ("They Ceased,"
"Devastaters," "It's Quiet with Man," and others) Uspensky
showed how reactionary attitudes influenced the mind and
behavior of the city and village dweller, and penetrated all
spheres of social, spiritual, and private life, destroying great

writers and artists. In his article, "Death of V. M. Garshin" ("Smert' V. M. Garshina") (1888), which in many ways explains Uspensky's own tragedy, Uspensky showed that the death of the Russian writer, Vsevolod Garshin, was caused not by pessimism or psychic dislocation as many had thought, but by social conditions which had "shocked his nerves and affected his whole spiritual life" (XI, p. 476).

In his letter (1888) to the publisher, V. Genkel, Uspensky wrote: "It's bad, it's painful to live in Russia now, and I would not advise even an enemy to lead such a life" (XIV, p. 91). In the same letter he said, "Russia, Russian life, and Russian thought are locked in a stifling store-room...."[20] "Social stagnation" was how Uspensky characterized the 1880's, a time when the country was ruled by a "stupid and base government" headed by Tsar Alexander III (XIV, p. 47).

In his struggle for justice and truth in social relations, for solidarity of the people, for freedom of the working masses, Uspensky placed great hopes in the *raznochintsy* intelligentsia, on whom he called to go and work among the people. He believed that "people of thought," whom he sometimes compared to saints of ancient times, would, as the educated, forward-looking people of his time, have a strong desire to turn their high ideals into deeds. This noble and Utopian hope, however, was shattered. Uspensky had also hoped to resist the power of "Mr. Dividend" by "divine means." By this he meant wise and just measures in the fields of credit, education, land ownership, tax assessment, and so on. But all this turned out to be dreams on paper. Uspensky also saw that the village community setup (*obshchina*) was incapable of defending the common people from the kulaks and landowners, from ruin and hunger. Uspensky had been attracted by many ideas and undertakings which seemed to him "salutary," but none withstood the test of time. The "divine truth" which he had hoped to see in human relations was mercilessly destroyed by the development of capitalism in Russia.

Writing became a tense and tormenting process for Uspensky. His thoughts on the subjects he was dealing with kept him in a constant state of tension and anxiety, and caused him to be extremely self-critical. Again and again he was overcome with a wish to make clear to himself exactly what was happening in

Russia and where she was heading, and whether his understanding of Russian life was correct. Since his hopes and deeds
turned out to be futile, he was led to a state of spiritual
exhaustion and crisis.

Here another important circumstance should be noted: Gorky
said that Russian literature suffered a great loss because Uspensky, the "wonderful person and highly talented writer, spent
too much time 'worrying and hurrying' and gave too much of
his energy to the poisonous 'bitter question of the day' without
looking into the future."[21]

Why did Gorky speak of the "poisonous" question of the
day? Why should concern about current problems have had
a negative effect on Uspensky? The answer is not merely that
Uspensky did not look into the future. He did. It is sufficient
to recall his conception of the image of Venus of Milo and his
sociological reflections evoked by Marx's letter for *Otechestvennye
zapiski.* One should keep in mind the following: To deal through
literature with the "bitter question of the day" was, under the
conditions of an exploiting society, a tormenting and—in the
final analysis—a fruitless undertaking, harmful to someone who
was socially conscious and who considered it his primary duty
to correct social evils through literary works.

Uspensky, absorbed by the most urgent questions concerning
the life of the people, constantly felt that his calls for justice,
truth, and social consciousness, his exposure of the wrongdoings
of the ruling classes, and his attempts to improve the life of
the common people had all failed. To give all of oneself for
the good of the people, to place one's talent and mind at the
service of the people, and yet not to see the desired results—
what could be more tragic for such a unique person and talented
writer as Uspensky? Thus, his confession is understandable:
". . . I am tired of peasants . . . and in general, of all those who
are cold and hungry. It is painful to look at this; and my head
refuses to suffer for this. I'm simply tired . . ." (XIV, p. 131).

In his letters of the 1880's and early 1890's Uspensky constantly spoke about his difficult situation, his feeling of oppression,
the lack of sympathy for his social and moral views, and his
doubts about his ability to continue writing. Uspensky, as noted
by his contemporaries, greatly admired the active fighters against
evil and was fascinated with the idea of self-sacrifice. In 1884,

during the trial of Vera Figner, Uspensky relayed a message to her, saying how he envied her (XVII, p. 630). Many questions arose before him: Was he or was he not a revolutionary? Was he capable of turning his words into deeds and sacrificing himself? Or was he scared and preferred not to risk his neck but to remain in Chudovo and "write once in a while?" (XIV, pp. 23, 24). It disturbed Uspensky that he was not able to act as a revolutionary and to be with those who led battles and sacrificed their lives for the freedom of the people. "Everything is taken away from me: there remains only my debt to all of those revolutionaries, the impossibility for me to be with them, the utter impossibility.... There remains emptiness, cold, and anxiety about everyday needs..." (XIII, p. 398).

To overcome his personal weakness and to enter into active struggle was a matter of life and death for Uspensky. He felt that because of the circumstances of his life and his personal character, he was unable to be a revolutionary. This gave rise to a morbid melancholy and the bitter feeling of guilt with respect to the revolutionaries, a wish to get out of his "skin," of all that pulled him back, and to become an "ideal Gleb"— someone who would be able to live and work with the best people of the country—with the saintly sufferers and revolutionary fighters. The split of his personality into two opposing parts was his torment in the years of his insanity.

Uspensky was sometimes overcome by a silent despair. He tried to forget everything by devoting himself entirely to literary work, to get away from his family whose egoistic attitudes oppressed him, to go to Siberia or abroad, to find employment, and "to come to his senses and leave aside literary work" (XIV, pp. 286, 287).

He was deeply moved on the occasion of the twenty-fifth anniversary (1887) of his entering the field of literature, an occasion widely marked by democratic circles in Russia. One of the many letters of congratulation he received was sent from the southern part of Russia and signed by 1279 persons, among them, many workers. In the letter, Uspensky was called "one of the best representatives of the 1860's." The letter said in part:

You have not embellished the bitter reality, you have not covered up social evils, you did not compose idylls about peasants and the village. . . . You forced us to shudder and be sick in our soul . . . and to look with courage into the future.[22]

By workers, peasants, and progressive intellectuals Uspensky was hailed as the "most honest son of his country," "a great writer and friend of the people," "a friend and teacher never to be forgotten," "one who felt great sorrow for the Russian soil." Uspensky's calls for working among the people and for the people were not futile. According to one letter signed by a number of persons (the letter is now in the Pushkin House archives), Uspensky's works taught that "people are everything," that "everything is for the people and that there is nothing without people."[23]

Uspensky was particularly struck by a letter from fifteen workers, members of a self-teaching group in Tiflis. In them Uspensky finally found the readers whom he had sought so long and with such anxiety. "Where is my reader?" he once asked, "I don't see him . . . a wall! I am throwing words, thoughts, my soul against a wall. I hear no response. . . . Does he need this? And who is he? Who?"[24] The letter from the Tiflis workers was an answer to these questions, a recognition of the importance of Uspensky's works. "When we read your stories," wrote the Tiflis workers,

we felt in our heart that you love us, that you love to tell the simple truth, and because of this we love you and your books. . . . And from these good books we were able to find much that is useful; we learned to think about our life and about our comrades . . . We learned to differentiate between good and evil, between truth and falsehood.

The workers said that Uspensky had helped them with his "compassionate words to reach out for light." They expressed the wish that their "dear" and "beloved" writer would live to see the "bright time—our joy," "the holiday of the long-suffering working people."[25]

The letter was a comfort and an inspiration for Uspensky in the darkest period of his literary and personal life. In his reply (published in *Obshchestvo lyubitelei rossiiskoi slovesnosti*, February 6, 1888) to the messages of greetings he had received, he mentioned this letter from the Tiflis workers and called on Russian writers to serve the new workers-readers (X_2, pp. 335ff.).

But Uspensky's spiritual torment did not end. He felt that he no longer had the strength to solve new problems and to do work that corresponded to the great and complex problems of life. This further deepened his anxiety. He felt "sickened and terrified" and "dry and cold" to live in the world. He spoke about his helplessness as a writer: "... I will no longer be able to write anything worthwhile; the sources are gone ...," "I have nothing to write about besides the story of a 'fierce sorrow.'" Uspensky felt that the tendencies of the time were pushing him aside: "the ugliness of the present" and the "endless darkness" depressed him. Sometimes he would say that he knew nothing, except the words "to suffer" and "one must not," that he was "plagued" by the village, by St. Petersburg, and by his family.

The defeat of the revolutionary movement; spying and exiles; censorship; the closing down of *Otechestvennye zapiski;* the forced retirement of his friend Saltykov-Shchedrin from the literary field and later—his death; disorder in the field of journalism and literature; personal financial difficulties; dependence on the liberal journal *Russkaya mysl* which he disliked; the necessity of working at a feverish pace in order to make a living—all made it difficult for Uspensky to work and led to his emotional collapse. Khristina D. Alchevskaya (a well-known figure and author of the book, *What People Should Read*) described Uspensky of those years as "a tall, thin man, with a sunken chest and a pale face full of suffering, and with beautiful, deep, and sad eyes which one never forgets after having seen them." "It seemed to me," continued Alchevskaya,

that in those eyes was reflected, as in a mirror, the suffering of all his life, the suffering of the people which he described so well. My heart became filled with an infinite sorrow, with a feeling that this man had but a few days left, that a serious illness was stealing up on him. . . .[26]

An indirect cause for Uspensky's emotional breakdown was the hunger in the Volga region covering twenty provinces in 1891-99. Uspensky took an active part in the publication of the book, *Aid to the Hungry* (1892), including raising money for the publication. Hunger, he said, "eclipsed" all his themes. His essays "Without Bread" (1891) and "Lamentable Times" (1891-

92) show that Uspensky was deeply shaken by the hunger in the Samara region caused not only by a bad harvest, but also by social and economic conditions there. In the fragment, "From a Notebook," Uspensky linked his stay in the Kolmovskaya mental hospital to the hunger in Russia.[27] Uspensky described the hopelessness of the economic situation of the peasants ("Rules of the Samara District" [zemstvo]) (1892). Peasants were heavily in debt and would never be able to pay back their debts ("What Will Happen Next?") (1892).

Uspensky died on March 24 (April 6 according to the old calendar), 1902. He was buried in the Volkov Cemetery next to Saltykov-Shchedrin.

Uspensky spent about ten years in hospitals before his death. During this period his works remained popular. His death was noted by the entire Russian press. His funeral was turned into a political demonstration. The writer V. V. Timofeeva-Pochinkovskaya, a friend of Uspensky's family, wrote in her memoirs:

The church, the streets, and the cemetery were filled with people. And what a strange stream of people who looked as if they were specially selected! . . . Nervous, spirited, but weak and tired-looking, with sullen and tense faces, emaciated, pale . . . and somehow noble and proud. . . . They were all dressed alike, in black or something dark, simply, without any attempt to be fashionable, who looked as if they did not care how they were dressed. The conversations were also strange. One could hear recollections about Siberia, the taiga, and prison. . . . A crowd of *raznochintsy* looking "nobly hungry" like the one they were burying, who had no ranks or titles, were marked by the police as "unreliable," "banished by the government," "pardoned," "a past criminal and may be one again in the future," "an unknown fugitive who had fearlessly come here to pay his last respects to the lamenter of people's suffering, who is under threat of being arrested"—these were the people who made up the majority of the crowd of several thousand. It was like a special nation with its own cult, its own principles and traditions, with its own secret language not understood by the uninitiated. . . .[28]

In Lieu of a Conclusion: Uspensky's Realism

> "The time will come when poetry will include
> ... moments of joy, hours of happiness ... an
> art will be born that will serve as a setting
> for those moments, like diamonds, and then
> they will sparkle both in books and in life."

USPENSKY was one of those writers who created a restless art of the written word, who took an active position with respect to the future, and who foresaw the possibility of exerting influence on life through literature. Uspensky was a writer who reproduced life as a natural-historical process and at the same time passionately fought to intervene in this process. In his cycle of sketches, *Willy-Nilly*, he wrote:

I am tormented and I suffer, and I want to torment the reader and make him suffer, because this resolution will eventually give me the right to speak about the most urgent and the greatest torments experienced by the reader himself. (XIII, p. 373)

It is necessary to underline Uspensky's position as an artist and publicist, his wish to look into the "infinitely bright future," and his attempt to attack courageously the reality of his time. This position led him to paint realistic pictures. Especially noteworthy is Uspensky's method of constructing cycles of sketches and stories in which descriptions of the hardships of the people and dreams about a happy and free life follow one another. Thus, there are two streams of narratives; one is dreamlike and the other realistic. Nearly all of Uspensky's cycles of travel notes and stories about the life of the people (*Letter From a Journey, Visits to Migrants, From Orenburg to Ufa— Ot Orenburga do Ufy*) follow this pattern.

Their structure is based on a comparison between the actual life of the people and what lay hidden in that life—what that life could become, the ideal life. Into the sad stories about the sufferings of the people are introduced beautiful descriptions of nature, poetic descriptions of labor—not back-breaking labor,

155

but work that reflects the "beauty of human living," his state of health, the "joy of being alive in this world" (see sketch "Laboring Hands" from the cycle *Letter from a Journey*). This contrasting of pictures—the real and the ideal—indicates Uspensky's keen awareness of the gap between them.

Compared with Vladimir Korolenko, Uspensky is more restrained in tone and has less tendency to write in a "dreamlike manner." It was time, said Uspensky, "to stop being carried away by dreams ... and to know the situation of the real, not dreamed-up, inhabitant of these bewitching deserts. ... It is necessary not to give the imagination of the reader the slightest chance to commit the great sin of dreaming ..." (XI, p. 176). Uspensky did not abandon "views of the distant future" (this is shown by the notes of Tyapushkin in *Vypryamila*), but he did not consider his main task—as did Korolenko—to be that of portraying what was bright and of bringing joy and dreaming. "But there is nothing else one can do ..." said Uspensky, "real life shouts so loudly about the absence of truth and about evil that it is absolutely impossible not to hear this howl, impossible to clam oneself with fantasies. One must speak of that which reality shouts about" (X₁, p. 326).

Uspensky turned to the sufferings of the masses, which were also his own constant sufferings. To continue to write about the life of the people in the same manner was already impossible for Uspensky. He had exhausted all the possibilities of this type of writing. Then, too, a new epoch had arrived—the end of the nineteenth century—when a new social force, the working class, appeared in Russia. A new approach to the life of the people was called for. Korolenko, who was of the younger generation, began to sense this. To the principle of Uspensky ("to speak of that which reality shouts about"), he added a new element which may be called the "Romantic symbol," which in different ways also began to enter the Realistic art of Garshin, Korolenko, and Chekhov. Thus began the transition from the old school of critical Realists to which Uspensky belonged, to a new trend in Realism as seen in the writings of his younger contemporaries. In these writings new aspects of Russian life were portrayed, and from their depths suddenly sparkled the "diamonds" about whose appearance in life and art Uspensky had only dreamed.

The Russia of Uspensky was becoming a thing of the past.

The author of *The Manners of Rasteryaeva Street* and *The Power of the Soil* had to grope in the dark; he lived and created in the epoch of Utopian socialism. His unattainable ideal of a holy life, based on the labor of one's own hands, led to spiritual and emotional breakdown. In *Talks About Trade*, Gorky said that it was the search for "divine truth" that caused Uspensky to become insane.[1] Uspensky is one of the most tragic figures in the history of Russian Utopian Peasant Socialism and in nineteenth-century Russian literature. He was literally crushed by the burden of his search for a bright life.

It would be impossible to understand the Russia of Uspensky's time, her difficulties and problems, or the meaning of the search of the progressive and revolutionary intellectuals of the time without understanding Uspensky's personality, without knowing his works in which the sufferings and pain, the hopes and illusions of a whole generation of the best sons of Russia were revealed.

Uspensky's spiritual tragedy was not meaningless. It pointed to the road leading to a new outlook, to different ways of life, different ideals. Uspensky himself was not pessimistic about the fate of his country. He did not fall into the state of hopelessness and pessimism which engulfed the intelligentsia of the 1880's and which can be seen in the writings of the philosopher, Vladimir Solovyov. After reading Solovyov's article entitled "Russia and Europe" which appeared in *Vestnik Evropy* (No. 2, 1888), Uspensky started writing an article called "A Bit of Something That's Good," which he did not finish. In the unfinished work Uspensky contrasted Solovyov's pessimism to the ideal of historical progress. Uspensky spoke about the misery of Russian life, about the "dark night" which sometimes became the "Black prison" and killed every "thought about something good, even a little of it." But he rejected the dark nihilism and fruitless skepticism of Solovyov, who saw no future for Russia and who passed the death sentence, as it were, on the Russian people (X_2, pp. 437-38).

Much can be learned from the life of Gleb Uspensky by generations coming after him. He lived and worked with great hopes, great ideas, and great thoughts about the future. Deeply saddened by the sufferings of the people, he did not give up his dream of the triumph of the beautiful in life and in literature.

Notes and References

All books and articles given here and in the Bibliography are in Russian, with the exception of quotations from Marx and the last item in the Bibliography.

Foreword

1. Vladimir G. Korolenko, *Collected Works* (*Sobranie sochinenii*) —hereafter referred to as Goslitizdat (Moscow: Gosudarstvennoe literaturnoe izdatel'stvo), I, 352.
2. Korolenko, "Gleb Ivanovich Uspenskii" ("O Glebe Ivanoviche Uspenskim") in *G. I. Uspenskii in Russian Criticism* (*G. I. Uspenskii v russkoi kritike*). (Moscow and Leningrad: Gosudarstvennoe izdatel'-stvo khudozhestvennoi literatury, 1961), 316.
3. For contemporary Soviet studies on Uspenskii see: G. A. Bialyi, "Some Characteristics of the Realism of Gleb Uspensky" ("O nekotorykh osobennostyakh realizma Gleba Uspenskogo") in *Scholarly Notes* (*Uchenye zapiski*), published by Leningrad State University No. 229, from the series *Philological Science* (*Seriia filologicheskikh nauk*), No. 30, 1957; Nikita I. Prutskov, "The Originality of the Realism of Gleb Uspenskii" ("Svoeobrazie realizma Gleba Uspenskogo") in *Problems of Realism in 19th-century Russian Literature* (*Problemy realizma russkoi literatury XIX veka*) (Moscow and Leningrad: Izdatel'stvo Akademii nauk SSSR, 1961), 263-80; cf. N. Sokolov, *G. I. Uspensky: His Life and Work* (*G. I. Uspenskii: Zhizn' i tvorchestvo*) (Leningrad: Izdatel'stvo "Khudozhestvennaya literatura," 1968), 302 (a response to the polemics of N. Prutskov and G. Bialyi).

Chapter One

1. Korolenko, *Collected Works*, V, 314.
2. This organization is not to be confused with *Zemlya i volia* which existed in 1861-63.
3. Gleb I. Uspenskii, *Complete Works* (*Polnoe sobranie sochinenii*) (Moscow and Leningrad: Izdatel'stvo Akademii nauk SSSR—here-after abbreviated "AN SSSR,"—1954), XIV, 582. All references to Uspenskii's works in this study are taken from this edition: I-XIV,

159

1940-1954. The numbers "1" or "2" when used under the number
of the volume indicate Book One or Book Two in the given volume.

4. Gleb Fomich Uspenskii, Uspenskii's grandfather on his mother's
side, corresponded with Leo N. Tolstoi.

5. Maxim Gorkii, *A History of Russian Literature* (*Istoriia russkoi
literatury*) (Moscow: "Goslitizdat," 1939), pp. 256-57.

6. At that time the *Autobiography* was not published. It first
appeared in full in Nikolai K. Mikhailovskii's article "Literature and
Life" ("Literatura i zhizn'") published in the journal *Russkoe bogatstvo* (No. 4, 1902).

7. Vera N. Figner, *Complete Works* (*Polnoe sobranie sochinenii*)
(Moscow: Ob'edinennoe gosudarstvennoe izdatel'stvo, 1932), V,
277-78.

8. In the Manuscript Division of the Institute of Russian Literature (Pushkin House) of the U.S.S.R. Academy of Sciences, Section
313, part 5, No. 24.

9. Gorkii, *Collected Works* (*Sobranie sochinenii*) (Moscow:
Goslitizdat, 1953), XXV, 342. All references to Gorkii are from this
edition.

Chapter Two

1. This and other epigraphs cited in this study are taken from
Uspenskii's *Complete Works.*

2. Vissarion G. Belinskii, *Complete Works* (*Polnoe Sobranie
sochinenii*) (Moscow: AN SSSR, 1955), VI, 431.

3. Gorkii, *Collected Works*, XXIV, 476.

4. *Ibid.*, XXV, 347.

5. See Prutskov, *Gleb Uspenskii in the Sixties* (Gleb Uspenskii i
shestidesiatye gody) (Tula: Oblastnoe knizhnoe izdatel'stvo, 1952),
p. 86. This work gives the factual background of *The Manners of
Rasteryaeva Street.*

6. Nikolai A. Dobroliubov, *Complete Works* (*Polnoe sobranie
sochinenii*) (Moscow: Goslitizdat, 1935), II, 231-32.

Chapter Three

1. For a discussion of the link between Uspenskii's works of
the first period and the plebeian novelists of the 1860's, see N. I.
Prutskov, *Questions of Literary-Critical Analysis* (*Voprosy litera-
turno-kriticheskogo analiza*) (Moscow and Leningrad: AN SSSR,
1960), p. 47ff.

Chapter Four

1. Kresty—a prison in St. Petersburg.

2. Cf. Ivan I. Popov, "Gleb Ivanovich Uspenskii" in *Studies of*

the State Museum of Literature. Gleb Uspenskii (Letopisi Gosudarstvennogo muzeia), Book 4, Moscow, 1939.

3. L. K. Chermak, "Reminiscences about G. I. Uspenskii," *Ibid.* I. I. Uspenskii (the writer's brother) and L. K. Chermak said that Uspenskii liked to have long talks with Beliaev. Chermak's description of Beliaev, the "genuine enthusiast about agricultural labor," resembles Uspenskii's portrait of Ivan Ermolaevich.

4. Gorkii, *Collected Works,* XXIV, 148.

5. Sviatogor-Bogatyr', a hero in Russian legends, is a symbol of great physical strength. Bogatyr' tried to find the "pull of the earth" in order to lift the whole earth.

6. See Prutskov, *Gleb Uspenskii in the Seventies and Early Eighties (Gleb Uspenskii v semidesiatykh—nachala vos'midesiatykh godov)* (Kharkhov, 1955), p. 112ff.

7. The publicist activity of the peasants was used by Uspenskii in his works: "A Peasant on Contemporary Events" ("Krest'ianin o sovremennykh sobytiiakh") (1882), "Village Correspondents and Publicists" ("Derevenskie korrespondenty i publitsisty") (1890), "Letters from Migrants" ("Pis'ma pereselentsev") (1891), and others.

8. On Uspenskii and T. M. Bondarev's pamphlet, see *Gleb Uspenskii. Material and Studies (Gleb Uspenskii. Materialy i Issledovaniia)* I, 283, 339-41; G. I. Uspensky, *Complete Works* (Moscow: AN SSSR, 1951), XIII, 623, 640-41.

9. Uspenskii, *Complete Works.* (St. Petersburg: Izdatel'stvo Tovarishchestva Marks, 1908), 6th ed., I, 17.

10. Nikolai K. Mikhailovskii, *Complete Works (Polnoe sobranie sochinenii)* (St. Petersburg, 1906), I, 166.

11. Leo N. Tolstoi, *Complete Works (Polnoe sobranie sochinenii)* (Moscow: Gosudarstvennoe izdatel'stvo khudozhestvennoi literatury, 1936), p. 346.

12. The author of this work is Lesnitskaia (pseudonym of V. I. Belenko).

13. See his letter to Uspenskii, Manuscript Department of the Institute of Russian Literature, Section 313, part 3, No. 35.

14. For details on this see Prutskov, *The Legacy of G. I. Uspenskii and the Literature of Socialist Realism (Nasledie G. I. Uspenskogo i literatura sotsialisticheskogo realizma)* in *Questions of Soviet Literature (Voprosy sovetskoi literatury)* (Moscow and Leningrad, 1955), III, pp. 168ff.

15. The article by Leo Tolstoi (part of a work which Tolstoi planned to write and which he entitled *What, Then, Should We do? (Tak chto zhe nam delat'?),* was written for the January issue of the journal *Russkaia mysl'* (1884), but its publication was forbidden by censorship. Uspenskii read the proof of the article.

16. Mikhail E. Saltykov-Shchedrin, *Complete Works* (*Polnoe sobranie sochinenii*) (Moscow: Gosudarstvennoe izdatel'stvo khudozhestvennoi literatury, 1937), XX, Book 3, 145.

17. Sergei N. Iuzhakov, "Questions of Hegemony at the End of the 19th Century," ("Voprosy gegemonii v kontse XIX veka), *Russkaia mysl*, No. 4, 1885.

18. *The Literary Legacy of G. V. Plekhanov* (*Literaturnoe nasledie G. V. Plekhanova*) (Moscow: Sotsial'no-ekonomicheskoe gosudarstvennoe izdatel'stvo, 1937), 4th ed., p. 186.

19. Leo N. Tolstoi, *Complete Works* (Moscow: Gosudarstvennoe izdatel'stvo khudozhestvennoi literatury, 1936), VIII, 346.

20. Figner, *Complete Works*, V, 468-69.

Chapter Five

1. Gorkii, *Collected Works*, XXX, 144.

2. *Gleb Uspenskii in Life* (*Gleb Uspenskii v zhizni*) (Moscow and Leningrad: Izdatel'stvo "Academia," 1935), pp. 182-85.

3. *Ibid.*

4. See V. Prytkov, *Nikolai Aleksandrovich Iaroshenko* (Moscow: Izdatel'stvo "Iskusstvo," 1960).

5. Iaroshenko's portrait of Uspenskii was used by L. V. Shervud for building the monument to the writer. The monument was unveiled on November 14, 1909 in Peterburg's Volkov Square.

6. *Sovremennik*, No. 2, 1857, pp. 265-67.

7. Afanasii A. Fet, *Complete Poems* (St. Petersburg, 1910), 2nd ed., I, 200.

8. Feodor M. Dostoevsky, *Complete Literary Works* (*Polnoe sobranie khudozhestvennykh proizvedenii*) (Moscow and Leningrad: Gosudarstvennoe izdatel'stvo, 1927), VII, 280.

9. Mikhailovskii, *Complete Works*, II, 610.

10. Dmitrii I. Pisarev, *Selected Works* (*Izbrannye sochineniia*) (Moscow: Gosudarstvennoe izdatel'stvo khudozhestvennoi literatury, 1935), II, 309.

Chapter Six

1. Gorkii, *Complete Works*, XXVII, 269.

2. The lines were taken by Uspenskii from the poem "Kosar' " ("Mower") by Alexei V. Kol'tsov.

3. Eruslan Lazarevich, hero of a Russian fairy tale, noted for his Herculean strength.

4. Uspenskii obviously had in mind the paintings by the well-known battle painter Vasilii V. Vereshchagin, "The Conquered"

("Pobezhdennye"), "Requiem" ("Panikhida po ubitym") and "Shipka-Sheinovo" (1878-79).

5. Mikula Selianinovich, a plowman of great physical strength in Russian fairy tales: "Mikula Selianinovich and the Pull of the Earth" ("Mikula Selianinovich i tiaga zemnaia"), "Volga and Mikula Selianinovich."

6. The miners' songs were written at the Donets Basin by the Populist writer S. A. Rappoport (pseudonyms: Semen Vid'bin, S. A. —skii) and included in his manuscript entitled *The Life of the Miners* (*Shakhterskaia zhizn'*), which Uspenskii tried to help get published. Uspenskii also had notebooks in which are recorded humorous workers' songs written by the poet I. Kuraev, who also collected folk songs.

7. See reply by Alexander I. Ertel in the Manuscript Department of the Lenin State Library.

8. Manuscript Department of the Institute of Russian Literature, Section 313, part 3, No. 242.

9. See E. G. Bushkanets, *Gleb Uspenskii and Volzhskii Vestnik* (*Gleb Uspenskii i Volzhskii vestnik*) (Kazan, 1957), p. 14.

10. *Saratovskii Listok,* No. 74 (April 2, 1902).

11. Here Uspenskii had in mind Leo Tolstoi as a teacher of life.

12. I. A. Vyshnegradskii, professor of mathematics and a stock dealer. In January, 1887, he was appointed Minister of Finance. His tax policy was based on the rule: "Put pressure on the taxpayer, and money will be found" ('Pozhmi platel'shchika—i sredstva naidutsia").

13. Mikhail N. Katkov, reactionary publicist of the nineteenth century; editor of the newspaper *Moskovskie vedomosti,* and publisher of the journal *Russkii vestnik.*

14. *Correspondence of K. Marx and F. Engels with Russian Political Leaders* (*Perepiska K. Marksa i F. Engel'sa s russkimi politicheskimi deiateliami*) (Moscow: Gosizdat-vo politicheskoi literatury, 1951), 2nd ed., pp. 221-22.

15. Vladimir I. Lenin, *Complete Works* (*Polnoe sobranie sochinenii*), I, 274-75.

16. Saltykov-Shchedrin, *Complete Works,* XVI, 225.

17. *Ibid.,* XIII, 49.

18. *Gleb Uspenskii in Russian Criticism,* p. 228 (See "Foreword," note 2).

19. *Ibid.,* p. 345.

20. E. Letkova, *About Gleb Ivanovich Uspenskii* (*Pro Gleba Ivanovicha Uspenskogo*) in *Zven'ia,* Collection V, p. 698.

21. Gorkii, *Complete Works,* XXV, 317.

22. In the Manuscript Department of the Institute of Russian

Literature, Section 313, part 7, No. 131. Some of them have been published in *Gleb Uspenskii. Material and Studies* (Moscow and Leningrad: AN SSSR, 1938), p. 336ff.

23. *Ibid.*, Section 313, part 3, No. 398. The letter is dated "1893."

24. E. Letkova, *op. cit.*, p. 727.

25. *Gleb Uspenskii. Material and Studies*, I, 366-70.

26. Khristina D. Alchevskaia, *Thoughts and Experiences (Peredumannoe i perezhitoe)* (Moscow, 1912), p. 118.

27. Manuscript Department of the Institute of Russian Literature, Section 313, part 1, No. 173.

28. *Gleb Uspenskii in Life*, p. 545.

Uspenskii's Realism

1. Gorkii, *Complete Works*, XXV, 347-48.

Selected Bibliography

PRIMARY SOURCES

USPENSKII, GLEB I. *Polnoe sobranie sochinenii,* 14 vols. (Moscow and Leningrad: Izdatel'stvo Akademii nauk SSSR—hereafter referred to as AN SSSR—, 1940-1954).
————. *Sobranie sochinenii,* 9 vols. (Moscow: Gosudarstvennoe izdatel'stvo khudozhestvennoi literatury, 1955-1957).

SECONDARY SOURCES (*in Russian*)

Bol'shaia sovetskaia entsiklopediia, 2nd ed., Vol. 44, p. 384. (Article on Gleb I. Uspenskii.)
BUSH, V. V. *Literaturnaiia deiatel'nost' Gleba Uspenskogo* (Leningrad: AN SSSR, 1927).
CHESHIKHIN-VETRINSKII, V. *Gleb Ivanovich Uspenskii.* (Moscow: Izdatel'stvo "Federatsiia," 1929).
GLAGOLEV, N. A. *Gleb Ivanovich Uspenskii.* (From a course of lectures on the history of nineteenth century Russian literature.) (Moscow: Izdanie Moskovskogo universiteta, 1953).
Gleb Uspenskii. *Materialy i issledovaniia. I.* (Moscow and Leningrad: AN SSSR, 1938).
Gleb Uspenskii. Letopisi Gosudarstvennogo literaturnogo muzeia, Book 4 (Moscow, 1939).
G. I. Uspenskii v russkoi kritike (collection of articles) (Moscow and Leningrad: Gosudarstvennoe izdatel'stvo khudozhestvennoi literatury, 1961).
Gleb Uspenskii v zhizni (collection of articles). (Moscow and Leningrad: Izdatel'stvo "Akademiia," 1935). Memoirs, correspondence, and documents.
Istoriia russkoi kritiki, 2 vols. (Moscow and Leningrad: AN SSSR, 1956), Chapter 11, Vol. II, "Gleb Uspenskii—kritik."
Istoriia russkoi literatury, Vol. IX, "Gleb Uspenskii (Moscow and Leningrad: AN SSSR, 1956).
Istoriia russkogo romana, 2 vols. (Moscow and Leningrad, Izdatel'stvo "Nauka," 1964. Chapter XI, "Narodnicheskii roman").
PRUTSKOV, NIKITA I. *Nasledie Gleba I. Uspenskogo i literatura sotsialisticheskogo realizma.* In *Voprosy sovetskoi literatury,* Vol. III (Moscow: AN SSSR, 1956).

165

————. *Tvorcheskii put' Gleba Uspenskogo.* (Moscow and Leningrad: AN SSSR, 1958).

——˘——. *V. I. Lenin o Glebe Uspenskom.* In *Uchenye zapiski Instituta mirovoi literatury imeni A. M. Gor'kogo* (Moscow: AN SSSR, 1952). Vol. I.

Riabov, I. *Gleb Uspenskii. Kritiko-biograficheskii ocherk* (Moscow: Goslitizdat, 1954).

Sokolov, N. I. *G. I. Uspenskii, zhizn' i tvorchestvo.* (Leningrad: Izdatel'stvo "Khudozhestvennaia literatura," 1968).

————. *Masterstvo G. I. Uspenskogo.* (Leningrad: Izdatel'stvo "Sovetskii pisatel'," 1958).

SECONDARY SOURCES (*in English*)

Wortman, Richard. *The Crisis of Russian Populism.* (Cambridge: Cambridge University Press, 1967).

About the Author

Dr. Nikita I. Prutskov is chairman of the department of nineteenth- and early twentieth-century Russian literature at the Institute of Russian Literature (Pushkin House) of the Academy of Sciences of the USSR. Dr. Prutskov has published many works on Russian writers and critics of the nineteenth and twentieth centuries, including Gogol, Belinsky, Herzen, Goncharov, Uspensky, Zlatovratsky, Leskov, Chekhov, Dostoevsky, Kuprin, Pisemsky, and Grigorovich. He is also the author of *Classical Russian Literature and Our Time* and *Questions of Literary Criticism*—theoretical studies dealing with the philosophical, sociological, and esthetic aspects of nineteenth-century Russian literature.

Index

(The works of Gleb Uspensky are listed under his name.)

169